Sarah Reynard Thumm

"Let us sail on and see something of
the world," said Tatterhood.

STORIES OF MAGIC AND ADVENTURE

TATTERHOOD

AND OTHER TALES

Edited by Ethel Johnston Phelps

With Illustrations by Pamela Baldwin Ford

THE FEMINIST PRESS

LIBRARY OF CONGRESS CATALOGING IN PUBLICATION DATA
Main entry under title:
Tatterhood and other tales.
     SUMMARY: A collection of traditional tales from Norway, England, China, and many
other countries.
     1. Tales. [1. Folklore. 2. Fairy tales] I. Phelps. Ethel Johnston. II. Baldwin-Ford, Pamela
PZ8.1.T162   398.2   78-9352   ISBN 0-912670-49-5   ISBN 0-912670-50-9 pbk.

For
Rachael, Jenny, and Nancy,
who love tales
of magic and adventure

TABLE OF CONTENTS

List of Illustrations ◎ *ix*
Preface ◎ *xi*
Acknowledgments ◎ *xiii*
Introduction ◎ *xv*

Tatterhood ◎ *1*
Unanana and the Elephant ◎ *7*
The Hedley Kow ◎ *13*
The Prince and the Three Fates ◎ *17*
Janet and Tamlin ◎ *23*
What Happened to
Six Wives Who Ate Onions ◎ *29*
Kate Crackernuts ◎ *33*
Three Strong Women ◎ *39*
The Black Bull of Norroway ◎ *49*
Kamala and the Seven Thieves ◎ *55*
The Giant Caterpillar ◎ *61*
The Laird's Lass and the Gobha's Son ◎ *65*
The Hunted Hare ◎ *79*
The Young Head of the Family ◎ *83*
The Legend of Knockmany ◎ *87*
Kupti and Imani ◎ *93*
The Lute Player ◎ *103*
Clever Manka ◎ *109*
The Shepherd of Myddvai and
the Lake Maiden ◎ *115*
The Search for the Magic Lake ◎ *121*
The Squire's Bride ◎ *129*
Wild Goose Lake ◎ *133*
Bucca Dhu and Bucca Gwidden ◎ *139*
The Enchanted Buck ◎ *143*
Mastermaid ◎ *149*

Notes on the Tales ◎ *157*
Suggested Reading ◎ *165*

LIST OF ILLUSTRATIONS

"Let us sail on and see something of the world,"
said Tatterhood. ◎ *frontispiece*

Inside the elephant's stomach, Unanana
began to feed her children. ◎ *11*

Janet dug her fingers into the bear and hung on
with all her might. ◎ *27*

Maru-me began to walk and, though the wrestler
tugged and pulled, he had to follow. ◎ *43*

"We women shall go and
kill the caterpillar!" they cried. ◎ *63*

"No, indeed," the old woman said firmly. "I saw
no hare run past me." ◎ *81*

Imani passed through the market crying,
"Medicine for sale!" ◎ *99*

The Lake Maiden entered the lake, her fairy
cattle behind her. ◎ *119*

"We will sing to the eagle,"
said Sea Girl. ◎ *135*

PREFACE

The tales in this book are old stories about magic and adventure. They are stories that ordinary people in the past told to entertain their families and friends. The stories were not originally thought of as "children's tales," but generations of children have loved hearing them.

The people in these tales do not behave the way girls and boys, women and men, have usually been expected to behave in real life and in stories. The heroes are not superior; they are human and vulnerable. The heroines have energy, wit, and sense.

Brief endnotes to each story tell those who are curious a little more about each tale. In the *Introduction,* there is more detailed information on the history and nature of folk tales; the *Notes* at the end of the book contain a discussion of the individual stories. There is also a brief list of tales suggested for additional enjoyment.

Seventeen of the tales have been retold by the editor. Eight have been retold by other writers. Many of these tales are over a thousand years old, and they have been continually retold—usually by women. Each generation of womenfolk passed on its stories to succeeding generations. In publishing these tales, retold again for today's young people, The Feminist Press is one more link in this chain of women storytellers.

ACKNOWLEDGMENTS

My sincere thanks to local librarians, too numerous to name, in the Nassau County Library System and to librarians in the Donnell Children's Branch (New York Public Library) for their help and enthusiastic interest in my project. I also want to express my appreciation for the guidance and unfailing support given by my editors at The Feminist Press, Corrine B. Lucido and Sue Davidson.

INTRODUCTION

The stories in this book were chosen for a special characteristic that singles them out from other folk and fairy tales.[1] They portray active and courageous girls and women in the leading roles. The protagonists are heroines in the true and original meaning of the word—heroic women distinguished by extraordinary courage and achievements, who hold the center of interest in the tales.

Active heroines are not common among the folk tales that survived by finding their way into print; and it is the printed survivals that are the main sources of the tales we know today. Since these tales come from the body of folk tale literature that began to be translated into English in the nineteenth century, they reflect a Western European bias. It is therefore not possible to say that the observations made here apply to all folk literature, but only to the published tales we have inherited.

The overwhelming majority of these tales present males as heroes, with girls and women in minor or subservient roles; or they feature young women like Cinderella and Sleeping Beauty, who passively await their fate. Only rarely, scattered among the surviving tales, do we find stories of girls and women who are truly heroines, who take the leading part and solve the problems posed by the adventure. It must be remembered, of course, that out of the enormous literature of oral folk tales, including every culture around the globe and reaching back well over a thousand years, many tales were lost during the centuries of verbal transmission. What proportion of these "lost" tales might have featured active heroines can only be a matter of conjecture.

[1] The term *fairy tale* is often used to refer to folk tales especially for children; to distinguish folk tales dealing with supernatural elements; to signify a tale revised or created by a known author. *Fairy tale* and *folk tale* are also used interchangeably. Since all the tales in this book are genuine folk tales, I have chosen to use that term.

The awakening nationalism of the nineteenth century brought a sudden surge of interest in the oral tales of the common people. Their tales were seen as a vanishing national heritage that should be collected and preserved. The Grimm brothers began this task with the publication of *Nursery and Household Tales* in 1812; other European and British scholars soon followed.

Only a few women published collections of local tales in the nineteenth century. Almost all the folk tale collectors of the period were well-educated males of a different social class from the rural storytellers they solicited. For Europeans collecting in Asia and Africa, the factor of color and race would be additional impediments to securing truly representative tales.

Folklorists Andrew Lang, George W. Dasent, and Stith Thompson, for example, wrote of the difficulties all folklorists experienced in collecting tales. Although women, particularly elderly women, were "the repositories of these national treasures" (a nation's folk tales) and the best sources of fairy and supernatural tales, some rural women were reported as unwilling to divulge their store of tales to the collector, for fear of ridicule. These reports referred to various areas of Europe, but the same note is made by Sarah F. Bourhill and Beatrice L. Drake, who published tales gathered in South Africa around the turn of the century. Among South African blacks, they noted, women were most often the village storytellers; however, the women told Bourhill and Drake that they feared ridicule if they told their tales to whites.[2]

Many women did, of course, recite their tales to collectors. But the reticence of some suggests, at the very least, that the tales they were willing to recite were probably those they felt would be socially acceptable and pleasing to the collector. Taking such factors into account, it seems likely that although the preservation and oral transmission of folk tales had for centuries been shared by rural women and men, a much smaller proportion of the tales women knew were collected, recorded, and published. The scarcity of heroic women and girls in the folk tales available today may be one consequence.

Nevertheless, women have always been deeply involved in preserving and transmitting this body of marvelously imaginative folk material. They enjoyed and retold the tales while working or at leisure. Their repertory was often large, and they performed with skill as storytellers, passing on the tales to succeeding generations of women. The phrase, "old wives' tales," now used derisively, takes on a new and

[2]*Fairy Tales from South Africa*, London, 1910, Introduction, p. v.

more positive meaning—for the "old wives' tales" were, indeed, the very rich and varied source of each nation's heritage of folk literature.

A few folk tales were published in the eighteenth century specifically for children, but it was not until the latter half of the nineteenth century that the tales definitely became a part of children's literature. Andrew Lang's many volumes of fairy tales attained great popularity. It is worth noting, in the present context, that although Andrew Lang selected the stories, it was Leonora Alleyne Lang, his wife, who translated, adapted, and retold for young readers the bulk of the collection, which eventually ran to over three hundred stories. Young women relatives and friends contributed the remaining tales. At the end of the preface to each of the books, Andrew Lang made specific acknowledgment of all these contributions. "My part," he wrote, "has been that of Adam...in the garden of Eden. Eve worked, Adam superintended. I also superintend....I find out where the stories are and advise."[3] However, Andrew Lang never saw fit to include his wife's name on the title page along with his own.

The Lang fairy tale books, like all collections of this kind, were retold tales, as are the tales in this collection. Adult readers are sometimes troubled by the retelling of folk tales, feeling that they should not be "tampered with." But which version of a tale is authentic, and what is meant by "tampering" is not altogether clear.

In fact, the one thing that is certain about traditional folk tales is that they have been constantly retold, with new tellers changing details and emphasis to suit both the times and the local audience. Most of the tales exist in many versions or variants, often appearing in different countries, sometimes in different areas of one country. There is no one "authentic" version of a folk tale.

While the stories in this collection are retold stories, they are all traditional folk tales. In editing and in some cases retelling these tales, my general purpose has been to sharpen and illuminate the basic story for the greater enjoyment of children today. Since the evocation of a faraway time and place is a large part of a tale's power to charm, I have kept to the style of the sources and retained much of their language, including old and obsolete words. In some stories, I have changed certain minor external details, but plot and characters are unaltered. Elements of violence or cruelty that serve no purpose intrinsic to the tale, however, have been omitted or moderated; similarly with unnecessary emphasis on remarkable physical beauty. Three of the tales,

[3]Andrew Lang, *The Lilac Fairy Book*, London, 1910, Preface, p. vii.

"Kamala and the Seven Thieves," "Mastermaid," and "The Prince and the Three Fates," I have edited down for the sake of a more compact story. The selections are varied in mood and style, from the leisurely early retellings of Lang ("Kupti and Imani") and Bourhill and Drake ("The Enchanted Buck") to the humorous modern versions of "The Laird's Lass" and "Three Strong Women."

In the distant past, the art of storytelling was a major source of community and family entertainment; and the tales were used and perceived in certain ways not central to present-day needs. Then as now, they offered a temporary escape from reality into the realm of fancy, distracting the mind and stimulating the imagination. Sometimes the tales served to explain or rationalize the terrors of the inexplicable and the unknown physical world. Because their themes echoed the accumulated experiences and beliefs of a people's past, they were capsules of folk wisdom, teaching and redefining moral and social values. Promoting messages by implication, rather than by obvious moralizing, they provided food for thought and discussion.

Encounters with the supernatural usually provide the action in these adventure tales. But whether the plot deals with supernatural creatures or humans, the problems posed test the character of the protagonists. Even though magic or wise advice may help them, it is their heroic qualities of courage or compassion, or their pluck or daring or wit, that enables them to combat successfully the varied forces of "evil." These forces may be greater or lesser, ranging from the cannabalistic giant in "Mastermaid" to the odious squire in "The Squire's Bride." Characteristically, folk tales imply that goodness will triumph over "evil."

Although the positive traits displayed by the successful protagonist still have meaning today, it is apparent that the social customs in the old tales, as well as some of their values, are outdated. How is it then that they continue to attract and entertain a contemporary audience? One answer is that a good adventure story dealing with the supernatural will always find an audience. The taste for adventures with the irrational and unknown, as well as the need for escape from reality, has not declined, but seems to fulfill a universal need in both adults and children. Some literary qualities of the folk tales, too, are timeless—the impudent humor of "The Legend of Knockmany" or "The Squire's Bride," for example. And in the underlying themes of the tales we find a comment on personal and social questions that still concern us: how couples conduct their relationships; how old women face threatening circumstances; how young men and women set about solving dilemmas perplexing to themselves or to the community. Although the themes are played out in a realm of magic spells, giants, fairies, and hobgoblins, the imaginative experience can be the yeast of creative thought that carries over to a more prosaic world. This, too, may be among the reasons that folk tales are one of the few forms of children's stories enjoyed by "children of all ages."

Folk tales also serve to provide a continuing link with the past, both in the sense of a heritage shared with many, and as a part of the individual's personal past—for it is usually the adult who enjoyed folk tales as a child who is eager to pass on to children the same enjoyment.

The emotional satisfaction children derive from the tales arises not only from the protagonist's achievement of success or good fortune against odds, but in seeing justice meted out to evildoers—as it often is to children themselves when they misbehave. Reassured by the traditional happy endings of fairy tales, children can delight in the perilous adventures.

Not all the tales that survive today exemplify the merits just discussed, nor do they meet with the wholehearted approval of parents and teachers. Cruelty and violence in the tales have been a subject of concern for some time. More recently, feminists have criticized the tales for their overemphasis on physical attractiveness, as well as the predominance of female characters who are meek and passive or heartlessly evil.

The danger—or value—of cruelty and violence in children's fiction is, of course, a controversial subject, encompassing television fare and comic books as well as classic literature. Among folk tale collectors, the Grimm brothers have been singled out most often for criticism of the goriness of their collections. It is useful to remember, however, that folk tales were originally shaped for an adult audience, and one that has long since vanished. Many of the descriptive details of folk tales reflect the period and the attitudes of the societies from which they sprang. These details are not sacred, nor does the alteration of them generally affect the basic theme, plot, and characters of the tale. What is important to a tale's meaning is that justice be done unambiguously—a consideration that does not invariably require adopting all of the retributive details of the source. It is not surprising that changed attitudes toward cruel and unusual punishments should influence choices among the tales and the way they are retold, as is the case with the selections in this book.

While feminist critics have raised objections to the convention of the heroine's surpassing beauty, there is not general agreement on this point. Some commentators suggest that the heroine's beauty is not the surface perfection of eyes, complexion, and hair, but the whole beauty of a joyous and radiant person, a symbol of inner beauty of character and personality. This interpretation of outer beauty, however, is an adult concept that may not be held by the average child; and certainly, for many children, it is discouraging to read that all heroines are extremely beautiful. More important, to be valued primarily for her beauty demeans the other qualities a heroine may possess. Although elements of extraordinary beauty, like those of extraordinary cruelty and violence, are an integral part of some plots, in many tales these are embellishments that can be dropped without affecting the story.

However, while it is possible to revise some elements of folk tales without destroying their integrity, the fact remains that the largest number of them portray girls and women unfavorably. We would not want all fictional images of women to be uniformly—and unrealistically—admirable. What is troubling is that although stereotypes of both sexes are common in folk tales, there is a marked pervasiveness of older women as frightening hags or evil crones, and of young women and girls as helpless or passive creatures. There are too few surviving tales of likable old women and active, resourceful young women to provide a balanced assortment. In the twenty-five tales in this book, you will encounter fifty or more characters of women and girls, and only two—the jealous mother of Kate Crackernuts and the malicious sister in "Kupti and Imani"—are lamentably undesirable characters. True, this redresses the balance with sheer force of numbers—but it is a balance that badly needs redressing.

Besides objecting to the folk tale conventions mentioned above, some adult readers question the relevance of the omnipresent queens, kings, princes, and princesses to the world of contemporary children. To children, however, as to the country folk who developed the tales, these rulers are symbols of might and wealth. As such, they represent power far beyond a child's command. At the same time, these royal beings move in a fanciful world easily entered by children, as by the rural audience that heard the tales.

For the queens, kings, princes, and princesses of the tales bear little resemblance to any royalty, then or now. Rather, they resemble the well-to-do landowner, farmer, and squire who were in fact the ruling class of the local countryside in Western Europe. Their actions and behavior are those of a prosperous landowner's family. A prince goes to the castle stable to saddle his own horse, a princess hires herself out as a menial servant, another is sent off to buy fresh eggs; a rajah listens to a poor barber's plea and gives him a piece of land—and so on. The "kingdoms" are very small, about the size of a village, and a day's walk often brings the protagonist to another "kingdom." This is a world not only within the grasp of the rural tellers—it is a world that a child's limited experience can comprehend.

The society depicted is usually simple; and in this simple, altogether fictional world, peasants and potentates intermingle and converse, moving apparently with little difficulty from one social level to another. Sometimes high rank or riches are achieved through cleverness, sometimes through an advantageous marriage. Whatever the specific device, it is the virtues and abilities of the protagonist that bring the material rewards so often included in the happy ending.

Marriage is also a traditional happy ending, and one that may appear outmoded measured by the standards of adults who wish to promote respect for the status of single persons of both sexes. Such a progressive view has in fact made headway, supported by the economics of an urban society. The tales, on the other hand, came out of the experience of a rural people concerned with problems of survival and the hopes and fears related to it. Marriage brought the establishment of one's own household and the continuity of offspring, conferring a settled place in the social and economic structure—all of which were necessary for rural survival and prosperity in earlier centuries. Thus, the marrying-and-living-happily-ever-afterward symbolizes all the material, social, and personal rewards achieved by the protagonist, whether male or female; to alter it in such cases would be to rob the tale of its meaning. The marriage ending reflects negatively on women in the general run of folk tales only because the "heroine" does little except sit, wish and wait for this goal, with no power over her fate and no active involvement in choosing or planning the circumstances of her future life.

The tales in this book describe many different kinds of heroines and heroes, but all the heroines, in one way or another, take on active roles and make decisions to shape their lives. It is this that sets them apart from the static "heroines" customarily found in folk tale collections. Out of the few surviving tales that give us true heroines, we have selected a gallery of strong, delightful women and girls for readers of all ages to enjoy.

TATTERHOOD

Once upon a time there was a king and a queen who had no children, and this grieved the queen very much. She was always bewailing their lack of a family and saying how lonesome it was in the palace with no young ones about.

The king remarked that if it were young ones she wanted running about, they could invite the children of their kinswoman to stay with them. The queen thought this a good idea, and soon she had two little nieces romping through the rooms and playing in the palace courtyard.

One day as the queen watched fondly from the window, she saw her two lassies playing ball with a stranger, a little girl clad in tattered clothes. The queen hurried down the stairs.

"Little girl," said the queen sharply, "this is the palace courtyard. You cannot play in here!"

"We asked her in to play with us," cried the lassies, and they ran over to the ragged little girl and took her by the hand.

"You would not chase me away if you knew the powers my mother has," said the strange little girl.

"Who is your mother?" asked the queen, "and what powers does she have?"

The child pointed to a woman selling eggs in the marketplace outside the palace gates. "If she wants to, my mother can tell people how to have children, when all else has failed."

Now this caught the queen's interest at once. She said, "Tell your mother I wish to speak to her in the palace."

The little girl ran out to the marketplace, and it was not

1

long before a tall, strong market woman strode into the queen's sitting room.

"Your daughter says you have powers, and that you could tell me how I may have children of my own," said the queen.

"The queen should not listen to a child's chatter," answered the woman.

"Sit down," said the queen, and she ordered fine food and drinks to be served. Then she told the egg woman she wanted children of her own more than anything in the world. The woman finished her ale, then said cautiously that perhaps she did know a spell it would do no harm to try.

"You must have two pails of water brought to you before you go to bed," said the egg woman. "In each of them you must wash yourself, and afterward, pour away the water under the bed. When you look under the bed the next morning, two flowers will have sprung up: one fair and one rare. The fair one you must eat, but the rare one you must let stand. Mind you, don't forget that."

The queen followed this advice, and the next morning under the bed stood two flowers. One was green and oddly shaped; the other was pink and fragrant. The pink flower she ate at once. It tasted so sweet that she promptly ate the other one as well, saying to herself, "I don't think it can help or hurt either way!"

Not long afterward the queen realized she was with child, and some time later she had the birthing. First was born a girl who had a wooden spoon in her hand and rode upon a goat. A queer looking little creature she was, and the moment she came into the world, she bawled out, "Mamma!"

"If I'm your mamma," said the queen, "God give me grace to mend my ways!"

"Oh, don't be sorry," said the girl, riding about on the goat, "the next one born will be much fairer looking." And so it was. The second twin was born fair and sweet, which pleased the queen very much.

The twin sisters were as different as they could be, but they grew up to be very fond of each other. Where one was, the

2

other must be. But the elder twin soon had the nickname "Tatterhood" for she was strong, raucous, and careless, and was always racing about on her goat. Her clothes were always torn and mud-spattered, her hood in tatters. No one could keep her in clean, pretty dresses. She insisted on wearing old clothes, and the queen finally gave up and let her dress as she pleased.

One Christmas eve, when the twin sisters were almost grown, there arose a terrific noise and clatter in the gallery outside the queen's rooms. Tatterhood asked what it was that dashed and crashed about in the passage. The queen told her it was a pack of trolls who had invaded the palace.

The queen explained that this happened in the palace every seven years. There was nothing to be done about the evil creatures; the palace must all ignore the trolls and endure their mischief.

Tatterhood said, "Nonsense! I will go out and drive them away."

Everyone protested—she must leave the trolls alone; they were too dangerous. But Tatterhood insisted she was not afraid of the trolls. She could and would drive them away. She warned the queen that all doors must be kept tight shut. Then she went out into the gallery to chase them. She laid about with the wooden spoon, whacking trolls on the head or shoulders, rounding them up to drive them out. The whole palace shook with the crashes and shrieking, until it seemed the place would fall apart.

Just then her twin sister, who was worried about Tatterhood, opened a door and stuck out her head to see how things were going. Pop! Up came a troll, whipped off her head, and stuck a calf's head on her shoulders instead. The poor princess ran back into the room on all fours and began to moo like a calf.

When Tatterhood came back and saw her sister, she was very angry that the queen's attendants had not kept better watch. She scolded them all around, and asked what they thought of their carelessness now that her sister had a calf's head.

"I'll see if I can get her free from the troll's spell," said Tatterhood. "But I'll need a good ship in full trim and well fitted with stores."

Now the king realized his daughter Tatterhood was quite extraordinary despite her wild ways so he agreed to this, but said they must have a captain and crew. Tatterhood was firm—she would have no captain or crew. She would sail the ship alone. At last they let her have her way, and Tatterhood sailed off with her sister.

With a good wind behind them, she sailed right to the land of the trolls and tied up at the landing place. She told her sister to stay quite still on board the ship, but she herself rode her goat right up to the trolls' house. Through an open window she could see her sister's head on the wall. In a trice, she leapt the goat through the window and into the house, snatched the head, and leapt back outside again. She set off with it, and after her came the trolls. They shrieked and swarmed about her like angry bees. But the goat snorted and butted with his horns, and Tatterhood smacked them with her magic wooden spoon until they gave up and let her escape.

When Tatterhood got safely back to their ship, she took off the calf's head and put her sister's own bonny head back on again. Now her sister was once more human.

"Let's sail on and see something of the world," said Tatterhood. Her sister was of the same mind, so they sailed along the coast, stopping at this place and that, until at last they reached a distant kingdom.

Tatterhood tied up the ship at the landing place. When the people of the castle saw the strange sail, they sent down messengers to find out who sailed the ship and whence it came. The messengers were startled to find no one on board but Tatterhood, and she was riding around the deck on her goat.

When they asked if there was anyone else on board, Tatterhood answered that, yes, she had her sister with her. The messengers asked to see her, but Tatterhood said no. They then asked, would the sisters come up to the castle for an audience with the king and his two sons?

"No," said Tatterhood. "Let them come down to the ship if they wish to see us." And she began to gallop about on her goat until the deck thundered.

The elder prince became curious about the strangers and hastened down to the shore the very next day. When he saw the fair younger twin, he promptly fell in love with her and wanted to marry her.

"No indeed," she declared. "I will not leave my sister Tatterhood. I will not marry until she marries."

The prince went glumly back to the castle, for in his opinion no one would want to marry the odd creature who rode a goat and looked like a ragged beggar. But hospitality must be given to strangers, so the two sisters were invited to a feast at the castle, and the prince begged his younger brother to escort Tatterhood.

The younger twin brushed her hair and put on her finest kirtle* for the event, but Tatterhood refused to change.

"You could wear one of my dresses," said her sister, "instead of that raggedy cloak and old boots." Tatterhood just laughed.

"You might take off that tattered hood and the soot streaks from your face," said her sister crossly, for she wanted her beloved Tatterhood to look her best.

"No," said Tatterhood, "I will go as I am."

All the people of the town turned out to see the strangers riding up to the castle, and a fine procession it was! At the head rode the prince and Tatterhood's sister on fine white horses draped with cloth of gold. Next came the prince's brother on a splendid horse with silver trappings. Beside him rode Tatterhood on her goat.

"You're not much for conversation," said Tatterhood. "Haven't you anything to say?"

"What is there to talk about?" he retorted. They rode on in silence until finally he burst out, "Why do you ride on that goat instead of a horse?"

"Since you happened to ask," said Tatterhood, "I can ride

*A kirtle is a skirt.

5

on a horse if I choose." At once the goat turned into a fine steed.

Well! The young man's eyes popped open wide, and he turned to look at her with great interest.

"Why do you hide your head beneath that ragged hood?" he asked.

"Is it a ragged hood? I can change it if I choose," she said. And there, on long dark hair, was a circlet of gold and tiny pearls.

"What an unusual girl you are!" he exclaimed. "But that wooden spoon—why do you choose to carry that?"

"Is it a spoon?" And in her hand the spoon turned into a gold-tipped wand of rowan wood.

"I see!" said the prince's brother. He smiled and hummed a little tune as they rode on.

At last Tatterhood said, "Aren't you going to ask me why I wear these ragged clothes?"

"No," said the prince. "It's clear you wear them because you choose to, and when you want to change them, you will."

At that, Tatterhood's ragged cloak disappeared, and she was clad in a velvet green mantle and kirtle. But the prince just smiled and said, "The color becomes you very well."

When the castle loomed up ahead, Tatterhood said to him, "And will you not ask to see my face beneath the streaks of soot?"

"That, too, shall be as you choose."

As they rode through the castle gates, Tatterhood touched the rowan wand to her face, and the soot streaks disappeared. And whether her face now was lovely or plain we shall never know, because it didn't matter in the least to the prince's brother or to Tatterhood.

But this I can tell you: the feast at the castle was a merry one, with the games, and the singing, and the dancing lasting for many days.

Peter C. Asbjornsen and Jorgen Moe collected this tale in the mid-nineteenth century, and G. W. Dasent translated it for his *Norwegian Folk Tales* (1859). The magic flowers, the goat, and the wooden spoon may be related to ancient superstitions and symbols. This retelling by the editor is based on Dasent's tale.

UNANANA AND THE
ELEPHANT

Many, many years ago there was a woman called Unanana who had two beautiful children. They lived in a hut near the roadside and people passing by would often stop when they saw the children, exclaiming at the roundness of their limbs, the smoothness of their skin and the brightness of their eyes.

Early one morning Unanana went into the bush to collect firewood and left her two children playing with a little cousin who was living with them. The children shouted happily, seeing who could jump the furthest, and when they were tired they sat on the dusty ground outside the hut playing a game with pebbles.

Suddenly they heard a rustle in the nearby grasses, and seated on a rock they saw a puzzled-looking baboon.

"Whose children are those?" he asked the little cousin.

"They belong to Unanana," she replied.

"Well, well, well!" exclaimed the baboon in his deep voice. "Never have I seen such beautiful children before."

Then he disappeared and the children went on with their game.

A little later they heard the faint crack of a twig and looking up they saw the big, brown eyes of a gazelle staring at them from beside a bush.

"Whose children are those?" she asked the cousin.

"They belong to Unanana," she replied.

"Well, well, well!" exclaimed the gazelle in her soft, smooth voice. "Never have I seen such beautiful children before," and with a graceful bound she disappeared into the bush.

The children grew tired of their game, and taking a small gourd they dipped it in turn into the big pot full of water which stood at the door of their hut, and drank their fill.

A sharp bark made the cousin drop her gourd in fear when she looked up and saw the spotted body and treacherous eyes of a leopard, who had crept silently out of the bush.

"Whose children are those?" he demanded.

"They belong to Unanana," she replied in a shaky voice, slowly backing towards the door of the hut in case the leopard should spring at her. But he was not interested in a meal just then.

"Never have I seen such beautiful children before," he exclaimed, and with a flick of his tail he melted away into the bush.

The children were afraid of all these animals who kept asking questions and called loudly to Unanana to return, but instead of their mother, a huge elephant with only one tusk lumbered out of the bush and stood staring at the three children. who were too frightened to move.

"Whose children are those?" he bellowed at the little cousin, waving his trunk in the direction of the two beautiful children who were trying to hide behind a large stone.

"They. . .they belong to Una. . .Unanana," faltered the little girl.

The elephant took a step forward.

"Never have I seen such beautiful children before," he boomed. "I will take them away with me," and opening wide his mouth he swallowed both children at a gulp.

The little cousin screamed in terror and dashed into the hut, and from the gloom and safety inside it she heard the elephant's heavy footsteps growing fainter and fainter as he went back into the bush.

It was not until much later that Unanana returned, carrying a large bundle of wood on her head. The little girl rushed out of

the house in a dreadful state and it was some time before Unanana could get the whole story from her.

"Alas! Alas!" said the mother. "Did he swallow them whole?
Do you think they might still be alive inside the elephant's
stomach?"

"I cannot tell," said the child, and she began to cry even
louder than before.

"Well," said Unanana sensibly, "there's only one thing to
do. I must go into the bush and ask all the animals whether
they have seen an elephant with only one tusk. But first of all I
must make preparations."

She took a pot and cooked a lot of beans in it until they
were soft and ready to eat. Then seizing her large knife and
putting the pot of food on her head, she told her little niece to
look after the hut until she returned, and set off into the bush
to search for the elephant.

Unanana soon found the tracks of the huge beast and followed them for some distance, but the elephant himself was
nowhere to be seen. Presently, as she passed through some
tall, shady trees, she met the baboon.

"O baboon! Do help me!" she begged. "Have you seen an
elephant with only one tusk? He has eaten both my children
and I must find him."

"Go straight along this track until you come to a place
where there are high trees and white stones. There you will find
the elephant," said the baboon.

So the woman went on along the dusty track for a very
long time but she saw no sign of the elephant.

Suddenly she noticed a gazelle leaping across her path.

"O gazelle! Do help me! Have you seen an elephant with
only one tusk?" she asked. "He has eaten both my children and
I must find him."

"Go straight along this track until you come to a place
where there are high trees and white stones. There you will find
the elephant," said the gazelle, as she bounded away.

"O dear!" sighed Unanana. "It seems a very long way and I
am so tired and hungry."

But she did not eat the food she carried, since that was for her children when she found them.

On and on she went, until rounding a bend in the track she saw a leopard sitting outside his cave-home, washing himself with his tongue.

"O leopard!" she exclaimed in a tired voice. "Do help me! Have you seen an elephant with only one tusk? He has eaten both my children and I must find him."

"Go straight along this track until you come to a place where there are high trees and white stones. There you will find the elephant," replied the leopard, as he bent his head and continued his toilet.

"Alas!" gasped Unanana to herself. "If I do not find this place soon, my legs will carry me no further."

She staggered on a little further until suddenly, ahead of her, she saw some high trees with large white stones spread about on the ground below them.

"At last!" she exclaimed, and hurrying forward she found a huge elephant lying contentedly in the shade of the trees. One glance was enough to show her that he had only one tusk, so going up as close as she dared, she shouted angrily:

"Elephant! Elephant! Are you the one that has eaten my children?"

"O no!" he replied lazily. "Go straight along this track until you come to a place where there are huge trees and white stones. There you will find the elephant."

But the woman was sure this was the elephant she sought, and stamping her foot, she screamed at him again:

"Elephant! Elephant! Are you the one that has eaten my children?"

"O no! Go straight along this track—" began the elephant again, but he was cut short by Unanana who rushed up to him waving her knife and yelling:

"Where are my children? Where are they?"

Then the elephant opened his mouth and without even troubling to stand up, he swallowed Unanana with the cooking-

Inside the elephant's stomach, Unanana
began to feed her children.

pot and her knife at one gulp. And this was just what Unanana had hoped for.

Down, down, down she went in the darkness, until she reached the elephant's stomach. What a sight met her eyes! The walls of the elephant's stomach were like a range of hills, and camped among these hills were little groups of people, many dogs and goats and cows, and her own two beautiful children.

"Mother! Mother!" they cried when they saw her. "How did you get here? Oh, we are so hungry."

Unanana took the cooking-pot off her head and began to feed her children with the beans, which they ate ravenously.

The elephant began to groan. His groans could be heard all over the bush, and he said to those animals who came along to find out the cause of his unhappiness:

"I don't know why it is, but ever since I swallowed that woman called Unanana, I have felt most uncomfortable and unsettled inside."

The pain got worse and worse, until with a final grunt the elephant dropped dead. Then Unanana seized her knife and hacked a doorway between the elephant's ribs through which soon streamed a line of dogs, goats, cows, men, women and children, all blinking their eyes in the strong sunlight and shouting for joy at being free once more.

The animals barked, bleated or mooed their thanks, while the human beings gave Unanana all kinds of presents in gratitude to her for setting them free, so that when Unanana and her two children reached home, they were no longer poor.

The little cousin was delighted to see them, for she had thought they were all dead, and that night they had a feast. Can you guess what they ate? Yes, roasted elephant-meat.

There is more than one version of this tale to be found among the tribes in the south of Africa. This story is reprinted from Kathleen Arnott's *African Myths and Legends* (1962).

THE HEDLEY KOW

There once was an old woman who earned her living by going on errands and doing odd work for the farmers' wives in the village where she lived. Although she earned only her midday meal and a bit of cheese and bread to bring home for supper, she was always as cheerful as if she hadn't a want in the world. Each day she rose early to gather branches and pine cones. These she laid ready near the hearth, and when she returned home to her cottage in the evening, she made a fire to keep herself warm.

Her cottage was small and poorly furnished. It stood by itself on the outskirts of the village, but she declared she was quite content to live alone, and she didn't mind the long walk home at all.

Nonetheless, the farmers' wives of Hedley made sure to send her on her way before sunset. After dark, the Hedley Kow* was abroad, and the Hedley Kow had terrified the villagers since times long past. Whether he was a bogie or a hobgoblin the village folk could not decide, but they did know he could assume fearful shapes and scare people out of their wits. He would chase them home, hooting and bellowing with raucous laughter, and other times he enraged them with all manner of mischief and pranks.

One summer evening as it was getting on toward dark, and the old woman hastened homeward, she came upon a big black pot lying at the side of the road.

*A kow is a bogie or hobgoblin, and probably pronounced *koo*.

"Now that," said she, stopping to look at it, "would be just the thing for me if I had anything to put into it! Who can have left it here?" She looked all around to see who it might belong to, but she could see no one either in the fields or on the road.

"Maybe it'll have a hole in it," said she. "Ay, that'll be how they've left it lying. But it'll do fine to put something in. I'm thinking I'll just take it home anyways." And she bent her stiff old back and lifted the lid to look inside.

"Mercy me!" she cried and jumped back. "If it isn't brim full of gold pieces!"

For a while she could do nothing but walk round her treasure, admiring the yellow gold and wondering at her good luck, and saying to herself, "Well, I do be feeling rich and grand!" But presently she began to think how she could best take it home with her. She couldn't see any other way than by fastening one end of her shawl to it and so dragging it after her along the road.

"I'll have all the night to think what I'll do with it," she said to herself. "I could buy a grand house and all, and live like a queen; or maybe I'll just bury it in a hole at the foot of the garden; or I could put a bit on the chimney near the teapot, as an ornament. Ah! I feel so grand I don't know myself rightly!"

By this time she was rather tired from dragging such a heavy weight, so she stopped to rest for a minute and turned to make sure her treasure was safe.

But when she looked at it, it wasn't a pot of gold at all, but a great lump of shining silver!

She stared at it, and rubbed her eyes, and stared at it again; but it was still a great lump of silver.

"I'd have sworn it was a pot of gold," she said at last, "but I reckon I must have been dreaming. Ay now, that's a change for the better; it'll be far less trouble to look after and not so easy stolen. Gold pieces are a sight of bother to keep safe. I'm well quit of them, and with my bonny lump of silver I'm as rich as can be!"

She set off homeward again, cheerfully planning all the

grand things she was going to do with the money. It wasn't long, however, before she got tired again and stopped once more to rest.

Again she turned to look at her treasure, and as soon as she set eyes on it, she cried out in astonishment. "Oh my! Now it's a lump of iron. Well, that beats all. It's real convenient—I can sell it as easy as easy, and get a lot of pennies for it.

"Ay, it's much handier than a lot of gold and silver that'd keep me awake nights, thinking I'd be robbed. A lump of iron is a good thing to have in the house; you never can tell what you might need it for."

So on she went again, chuckling to herself on her good luck, until presently she glanced over her shoulder just to make sure it was still there.

"Eh, what's this?" she cried as soon as she saw it. "It's gone and turned into a great stone! Now how could it know that I was just wanting something to hold my door open with? Ay, that's a good change. It's a fine thing to have good luck."

And all in a hurry to see how the stone would look in its corner by her door, she trotted off down the hill and stopped at the bottom beside her own gate.

Then she turned around to unfasten her shawl from the stone, which this time seemed to lie quiet and unchanged on the path. She could see the stone quite plainly as she bent her stiff back to untie the shawl end.

All of a sudden, it seemed to give a jump and a squeal, and grew in a moment as big as a great horse. It threw down four lanky legs, shook out two long ears, and flourished a tail. Then it kicked its feet into the air laughing raucously.

The old woman stared as it capered and shrieked and rolled its red shiny eyes.

"Well!" she said at last. "I do be the luckiest body! Fancy me seeing the Hedley Kow all to myself and making so free with it too!"

The Hedley Kow stopped short in its rearing and bellowing to glare at her. "You're not frightened?"

15

"Not me!" she laughed. "'Tis a rare sight you are!"

"Most folks shout and curse at me," said he, "ay, and run screaming!"

"There's no harm done," she answered cheerfully. "I still have my bit of cheese and bread for my supper."

She gathered her shawl about her and opened her little gate. But when she looked around, instead of the great gangling horse, there stood a small man in a pointed cap scuffling his feet on the path. He was brown as a russet apple, apart from his scraggly white beard.

"Well now," said the old woman kindly, "I don't have much, but you're welcome to come in for a bit of supper."

"Don't mind if I do," said the Hedley Kow.

So he sat down to supper with the old woman, and somehow the bit of cheese became a large chunk, and then there suddenly appeared on the table some nicely boiled brown eggs and crumpets for their tea.

They made a cheerful meal of it, and after they finished they sat beside the fire while the Hedley Kow regaled the old woman with stories of his pranks. She laughed until the tears rolled down her cheeks, and she declared that never had an evening passed so quickly.

As time went on, the little brown man came by often for a bit of supper and an evening of talk. And when the old woman found her woodpile always stacked high and her cupboard always stocked with food, she very wisely said nothing about it to anyone.

The village folk still talked fearfully of the Hedley Kow, or cursed him for his mischief, but the old woman would chuckle and say, "He be not that bad—happen he likes to kick up his heels a bit, he do!"

The "kow" or hobgoblin haunted the village of Hedley in the north of England. It never caused any serious harm but liked to frighten people and make mischief by changing shapes. This is a retelling by the editor of Joseph Jacob's nineteenth century version in *More English Fairy Tales* (1904).

THE PRINCE AND THE
THREE FATES

Once upon a time a little boy was born to a king and queen who ruled over a country on the banks of the great river Nile. The king and queen joyfully sent messages to all the most powerful peris, or fairy spirits, to come and see this wonderful baby. Within a short time, the fairy spirits were gathered round the cradle.

The king and queen were disturbed to see them look so grave.

"Is there anything the matter?" the king asked anxiously.

The peris all shook their heads at once. "He is a beautiful baby, and it is a great pity, but what is to happen will happen," said they. "It is written in the book of fate that he must die by either a crocodile, a serpent, or a dog. If we could save him we would, but that is beyond our power." And so saying, they vanished.

The king and queen stood horror-stricken at what they had heard. But being of a hopeful nature, they began at once to invent plans to save the prince from the dreadful doom that awaited him. A strong wall was built around their palace, and the child was guarded night and day.

One day, when the boy was six years old, he was sitting at a window when he saw a little dog running and playing outside the walls of the palace. He begged and begged for a dog of his own until the king, feeling sorry for the quiet life his son must lead, said, "Very well, let him have a puppy."

Years went by, and the boy and the dog played together till the boy grew tall and strong. The time came at last when he said to his father, "Why do you keep me shut up here doing nothing? I know all about the prophecy that was made at my birth, but I would far rather be killed at once than live an idle, useless life. Give me arms and let me go, I pray you, and my dog with me."

The king reluctantly granted his plea, knowing his son must now deal with his own fate. The prince and his dog were carried in the palace barge to the other side of the river. A black horse was saddled and waiting for him there, and he mounted and rode away wherever his fancy took him with the dog always at his heels.

Never was a prince so happy, and he rode and rode until at length he came to a great palace. There he found a number of suitors staying in the guest house on the palace grounds, for the princess of this land was being courted by many nobles and princes. She would not accept any of the suitors who thronged the palace, and told them all she was not ready to marry.

The prince was made welcome at the guest house with a perfumed bath, as was the custom, and invited to stay for a while. In due course he and the princess became friends, and soon their friendship ripened into love. The princess informed her father that she had made her choice.

At first the king hesitated, saying he knew little about this young man from another country. But the princess was firm; she would marry the prince or no one. So the marriage took place, and great herds of cattle and a large estate were given to the young couple.

A short time afterward, the prince told his wife of the prophecy made at his birth. "My life is in the hands of three creatures," he said. "I am fated to die by a crocodile, a serpent, or a dog."

"How rash you are!" cried the princess, throwing her arms around his neck. "If you know that, how can you have that horrid dog about you? He should be killed at once!"

"Kill my dog who has been my playfellow since he was a puppy?" he exclaimed. "Never would I allow that!" And all the princess could get from him was a promise that he would always wear a sword and have somebody with him whenever he left the estate.

When the prince and princess had been married a few months, the prince heard that his parents were ill, and longing to have their eldest son near them. The young man and his wife set out at once.

They spent the last night of the journey in a town on the banks of the great river. During the night, while the prince was asleep, the princess wakened to notice something strange in one corner of the room. It was a dark patch that seemed to grow longer and longer as it moved toward the cushions on which the prince was lying. She shrank in terror making a slight noise, but the creature heard it and raised its head to listen. Then she saw it was the long, flat head of a serpent, and the prophecy rushed into her mind.

Without waking the prince, she glided from her couch and, taking up a heavy bowl of milk which stood on a table, she laid it on the floor in the path of the serpent—for she knew that no serpent can resist milk. She held her breath as the snake drew near. Its eyes fell on the milk. In an instant it was lapping the milk so fast it was a wonder the creature did not choke. When every drop was gone, it dropped on the ground and slept heavily. This was what the princess had been waiting for. Catching up her husband's sword, she severed the snake's head from its body.

The next morning, after this narrow escape, they set out for the king's palace. Here they stayed for a long visit while the prince took over many duties of the kingdom from his father.

One morning, the prince went out with his bow and arrows and his dog to hunt wild duck. While chasing their game, they drew near the reed-covered bank of the river. The prince was running at full speed when he almost fell over something that looked like a log of wood. To his surprise a voice spoke to him, and he saw that what he had taken for a log was really a crocodile.

"You cannot escape from me," it said. "I am your fate, and wherever you go, whatever you do, you will always find me before you. There is only one way of shaking off my power. If you can dig a pit in the dry sand that will remain full of water, my spell will be broken. If not, death will come to you speedily. I give you this one chance. Now go."

The young man walked sadly away, and when he reached the palace he shut himself into his room. For the rest of the day he refused to see anyone, even his wife. At sunset, however, the princess grew alarmed and demanded to be let in.

"How pale you look," she cried. "Has anything hurt you? Tell me what is the matter for perhaps I can help!" So the prince told her the whole story and of the impossible task given him by the crocodile.

"How can a sand hole remain full of water?" he asked. "Of course it will all run through. The crocodile called it a chance; but he might as well have dragged me into the river at once. He said truly that I cannot escape him."

"Oh, if that is all," cried the princess, "I can set you free myself, for my nurse taught me to know the use of plants. In the desert, not far from here, there grows a little four-leaved herb which will keep the water in the pit for a whole year. I will go in search of it at dawn, and you can begin to dig the hole as soon as you like."

To comfort her husband the princess had spoken lightly and gaily, but she knew very well she had no light task before her. Still, she was full of courage and energy and determined that her husband should be saved.

It was still starlight when she left the palace on a snow-white donkey and rode away from the river straight to the west across the desert. For some time she could see nothing before her but a flat waste of sand, which became hotter and hotter as the sun rose. Then a dreadful thirst seized her and the donkey, but there was no stream from which to drink. So she spoke cheering words to her donkey, who brayed in reply, and the two pushed steadily on.

How glad they both were when they caught sight of a tall rock in the distance! They forgot that they were thirsty and the sun hot. The ground seemed to fly under their feet, till the donkey stopped of its own accord in the cool shadow. But though the donkey might rest, the princess could not, for she knew the plant grew on the very top of the rock, and a wide chasm or pit ran round the foot of it.

She had thought to bring a rope with her and, making a noose at one end, she flung it across with all her might. The first time it slid back slowly into the deep pit, and she had to draw it up and throw it, again and again, until at last the noose caught on a jagged point of rock. Now she had to trust her whole weight to the rope which might snap and let her fall onto the rock below. But nothing so terrible happened. The princess safely reached the other side, and then came the worst part of her task. As fast as she put her foot on a ledge or outcropping of rock to climb, the stone broke away and left her as before. Meanwhile the hours were passing, and it was nearly noon.

She tested several places on the rock face in this way before she found one place more solid than the rest. She managed by great effort to reach it and, finally, with torn and bleeding hands, she gained the top. There was such a violent wind blowing that, almost blinded with sand, she was obliged to throw herself on the ground and feel about for the precious herb.

For a few terrible moments she thought the rock was bare and her journey had been to no purpose. It seemed there was nothing but grit and stones, when suddenly her fingers touched something soft in a crevice. It was a plant, that was clear; but was it the right one? She could not see, for the wind was blowing more fiercely than ever, so she lay where she was and counted the leaves. One, two, three,—yes! There were four! And plucking it, she held it safe in her hand while she turned, almost stunned by the wind, to go down the rock.

When once she was safely over the side all became suddenly still, and she slid down the rock so fast that she almost landed in the pit. However, by good luck, she stopped quite close to her rope bridge and was soon across it. The donkey brayed joyfully at the sight of her and set off home across the desert at high speed, never seeming to know that the sand underfoot was nearly as hot as the sun above her.

On the banks of the great rivers she halted, and the princess hurried over to where the prince was standing by the deep hole he had dug in the sand. A huge clay waterpot stood beside him. A little way off, near the bulrushes at the river's edge, the crocodile lay blinking in the sun with his yellow jaws open and his sharp teeth waiting.

At a signal from the princess, the prince poured the water into the hole; and the moment it reached the brim the princess flung in the four-leaved plant. Would the charm work, or would the water trickle slowly through the sand? For half an hour they stood with their eyes fixed on the spot, but the hole stayed as full as at the beginning, with the little green leaves floating on the top. Then the prince turned with a shout of triumph, and the crocodile sulkily plunged into the river. The prince had escaped forever the second of his three fates!

He stood there looking after the crocodile and rejoicing that he was free, when he was startled by a wild duck which flew past them, seeking shelter among the reeds and rushes that bordered the river. In another instant his dog dashed by in hot pursuit and knocked heavily against his master's legs.

The prince staggered, lost his balance, and fell backward into the river, where the deep mud and reeds caught him and held him fast. He shouted for help to his wife who came running with the rope she had left coiled near the donkey. The poor old dog was drowned, but the prince was pulled to shore.

"My wife," he said to her gratefully, "has proved stronger than my fate."

This story is from the Sudanese region of the Nile River. Originally from a collection of ancient Egyptian tales, it was translated and adapted by Leonora Alleyne Lang for *Olive Fairy Book* (1907). The present retelling by the editor abridges her story to some extent.

JANET AND TAMLIN

Once upon a time in the lowlands of Scotland, there lived an old earl and his bonnie daughter, Janet. And on their lands, in the place called Carterhaugh, there stood from ancient times a well belonging to the fairy folk.

Now Janet had the freedom to go wherever she wished except for one place, and that place was the fairy well at Carterhaugh. Indeed, all the village lasses were warned not to tarry at Carterhaugh for it was believed the fairy knights would spirit away any young maid found near the well. Sometimes, village folk who must pass by Carterhaugh left offerings beside the well to please the fairies and bring good luck to themselves.

Janet longed to visit her fairy well to see what she could see. Perhaps she would leave an offering at the well and make a wish for good fortune. So one fine sunny morning she braided her hair about her head, tucked up her kirtle high above her knees, and hastened off to Carterhaugh as fast as she could go.

The green meadow was filled with the scent of heather and wildflowers, roses, and golden broome. Beside the well stood the ancient hawthorn trees, and there Janet hung a silver pin as an offering. She picked a wild rose to tuck in her hair and bent down to peer inside the dark cold water of the well. When she looked up, beside the well grazed a splendid white horse with golden trappings.

Janet moved away uneasily and picked two more roses for her girdle. But, then, standing before her was a young man clad in shimmering green.

"Why do you pick my roses, lady?" he demanded. "Why do you come to Carterhaugh without my leave?"

"Without your leave indeed!" cried Janet. "Carterhaugh is my father's land. I'll come here if I please!"

"The flowers are mine, lady. When you plucked the roses you summoned me."

"I'll pluck a rose if I wish," she answered with spirit. "Who are you to claim the flowers of Carterhaugh?"

"I am the knight, Tamlin, from the court of the Queen of Elfland."

"I am—Janet," she faltered, and grew afraid for all the warnings and fearful tales she had heard rushed into her mind.

Tamlin smiled gently. "I'll not harm you, Janet."

"Glad I am to hear it, for I've been forbidden to visit the fairy well." She went on ruefully, "It would be a sad thing indeed if they were proved right!"

"Will you tarry awhile, Janet?"

"I will," she said. So they sat and talked together in the fragrant meadow all that summer's day. When evening came Janet returned home, running lightly through the heather.

"No harm has come of it," she said to herself. But she found she thought only of Tamlin, and a few days later she was back at Carterhaugh picking the wild roses at the well. At once Tamlin appeared at her side.

After that Janet went often to the fairy well. Tamlin confessed he haunted the well, waiting for her summons, and Janet thought there was no place she'd rather be than at Carterhaugh with Tamlin.

As the summer waned into autumn, Janet grew sad and quiet. She realized she loved Tamlin, and to love a knight from Elfland was, she knew, a hopeless thing. The maids saw her moping and whispered that Janet had a lover. And her father noticed she was not like her usual merry self at all.

"What ails you, lass?" he asked kindly. "Is it dull here in the castle? Perhaps it's time that you were wed. If there's no young laird you fancy hereabouts, we'll go off to Edinbro' and see what we can find there."

But Janet just shook her head.

The very next day Janet hurried off to Carterhaugh, and when Tamlin stood beside her she said, "Tell me truly, Tamlin, are you mortal man or fairy spirit?"

"I was a mortal man," he sighed. "I was the Earl of Roxburgh's grandson. But one day riding on the hunt, my horse stumbled and I was thrown hard to the ground. 'Twas on a fairy hill, so as I lay stunned, the Queen of Elfland seized me and took me in to be her knight.

"I liked it very well at first. Now, since I've met you, Janet, I want to return to the real world. If I were free I'd ask your pledge to marry me."

"And I'd say yes," answered Janet. "Is there no way you can leave the fairy world?"

Tamlin shook his head sadly. "The Queen's enchantment is strong, and she has refused to let me go."

"I'll marry no one but you, Tamlin, and I'll not give you up easily. Is there no way to break the enchantment?"

"There's but one way to free me. It's a fearful way, and I doubt that any mortal lass could do it."

"I will do it," said Janet, "if you will tell me what it is."

"Next week comes Halloween. On that night the Queen and all her knights and company ride abroad. You must wait for us near the well at Miles Cross, but stay hidden; you must not be seen. At midnight we will be riding past. It is then you must run out and drag me from my horse."

"How will I know which is you among all that company, Tamlin?"

"Let the first group of three riders pass, and then the second. I will be in the third company. One knight will ride a black steed, the other a brown. But I will ride a pale grey steed on the outer side. My right hand will be gloved, my left hand bare. By this you will know me."

"I will be there," she promised.

"Run quickly to the grey steed and pull the rider down. The fairy host will raise the cry, 'Tamlin is away!' Hold me fast and do not let me go. They'll change me to a wild beast or a

25

snake, but you must hold me fast within your arms, no matter what terrible shape I take. Fear not, I'll do you no harm. They'll turn me into a red-hot bar of iron, and at the very last, they'll turn me into a burning coal. Then quickly throw the coal into the well water, and I'll become a human naked man. Cover me with your cloak and keep me out of sight until the fairy host are gone."

"I will do all that," said Janet. "I will not fail you, Tamlin."

An hour or two before midnight on Halloween, Janet quietly left the sleeping castle. The night was dark and gloomy, and the large branches of the ancient oaks creaked and groaned with the wind. She wrapped her cloak around her and set out for Miles Cross. The dry leaves on the path skittered and rustled as though they were alive. Dark shadows seemed to press around her as she hurried on.

When she reached the well at Miles Cross, she hid herself in the bracken and bushes nearby. Here there was no sound but the wind sighing through the trees. She waited so long she feared the fairy host would not be coming that night.

Then a little before midnight she heard the jingle of fairy bells on bridles. The music of the bells grew clearer, and the strange elfin glow of fairy folk showed her the Queen riding at the head of the fairy company. Her long golden hair gleamed as it lay over her shoulders and over her shimmering green mantle.

A company of three knights rode behind her, and behind them a second company of knights. Janet let them pass. In the third company were a knight on a black steed and a knight on a brown. The third knight, on the pale grey steed, rode on the outer side. His right hand was gloved, his left hand bare.

Janet ran out to the pale grey steed and caught the bridle. She seized hold of the knight and dragged him to the ground. From the fairy host a fearful shriek rang out: "Tamlin is away!"

She felt Tamlin shrink in her arms to become a slippery, wriggling lizard, but she held it fast. The lizard turned into a

Janet dug her fingers into the bear and
hung on with all her might.

scaly snake, twisting and coiling in her arms, but she did not let it go.

The snake became a lean wolf with wide snapping jaws, but she gripped it tightly in her arms and did not let it go. The wolf turned into a large shaggy bear with huge paws and sharp teeth. She dug her fingers into the fur and hung on with all her might.

The bear became a fierce lion with large fangs who threw her to the ground, but she held fast and did not let go.

Then the lion became a bar of red-hot iron in her hands. She gritted her teeth and staggered to her feet, but would not drop it. At last the iron bar became a glowing coal, and this she threw into the well.

A cry of rage went up from the fairy host. By the unearthly elfin light she saw Tamlin climb naked from the well and quickly threw her cloak over him, hiding him from their sight.

The Queen cried out angrily to Janet, "You have taken my best knight! If I had known Tamlin would be taken from me, I'd have turned his eyes to wood and his heart to stone!"

With that the fairy host rode off into the night, the eerie glow fading, the golden bridle bells jingling faintly in the distance.

In the silence and the dark, Janet crouched near the well still holding Tamlin closely in her arms. She knew that Tamlin was now free, and that he would be her heart's delight.

Several old ballads about Janet and Tamlin from the Border Country of Scotland were used by the editor as a source for this story. Tales of humans captured by the fairies or the Queen of Elfland are frequent in Celtic folklore, but not all end as happily as this one does.

WHAT HAPPENED TO SIX WIVES
WHO ATE ONIONS

Western Mono Indians lived high up on the Kings River. They knew how to use magic.

Here is a story they told:

Once there were six pretty Mono wives. These wives had six husbands who were mountain lion hunters.

One day, while the husbands were out hunting, the wives went up the mountain to pick clover for food. That day, one wife discovered something new to eat—wild onions.

"Yum, these new plants taste better than anything I've ever eaten!" she told the others. "Just taste this."

The other wives all tasted the onions. They liked them too. They ate and ate and smacked their lips and then went home to cook supper for their husbands.

Just as dusk was falling the husbands came plodding home. Each had killed a big mountain lion.

"Phew! What's the odor?" the husbands asked their wives when they got to the hut door.

They came closer to their wives and discovered the terrible odor was on the breath of their wives!

"We found this new plant to eat—just taste it." the wives said and offered some to the husbands.

"No!" they cried in disgust. "Your breath is enough for us —horrible!" They wouldn't even taste the onions.

That night the husbands made their wives stay outdoors because the odor of onions kept them awake.

It was cold outside and the wives didn't like to stay out there alone without their husbands.

The next day when the husbands had gone hunting, the wives went back to where the onions grew and ate more than they had the day before. Those onions were so tasty, they just couldn't help eating them.

When the husbands came home for supper, not one of them had slain a mountain lion. Never before had they come home without mountain lions and they were very sad.

"Mountain lions smelled that horrible odor on us," they grumbled. "Mountain lions ran away fast before we could get near enough to catch them."

The wives didn't believe their husbands and said so.

But when the husbands smelled the odor of onions stronger than ever, they scolded.

"You can't come near us! You are worse than skunks."

Again, they wouldn't let their wives come inside the hut to sleep. They wouldn't put food out for their wives to eat.

The wives went home to their fathers and mothers, but that didn't do any good. They were sent right back to their husbands.

This lasted six days. Each night the men came home without mountains lions and each night they found their wives had been eating onions again.

Finally, what with the strong odor of onions and not getting mountain lions, the husbands went into a terrible rage.

"Go away!" they shouted. "Go away! We can't hunt! We can't sleep nights because you eat so many onions. We don't want you any more. Go away!"

The next morning when the husbands had gone, the wives all went up the mountain to where onions grew. Each of them took her magic rope made of eagle's down.

They were hungry and missed the mush, and they were tired of sleeping alone in the cold outside the hut at night.

"Let's leave our husbands forever," one wife said. "Our husbands don't like us any more."

They all agreed.

So they climbed and climbed up a big rock. Each wife carried her eagle-down rope. One wife brought her little girl with her.

At last, they reached the very top of the rock. They rested awhile, then the leader of the wives said, "Now is the time for magic. Do you still want to leave your husbands forever?"

"Yes!" they all cried.

So the leader of the wives said a magic Mono word and threw her eagle-down rope up into the sky.

"Whosh!" it went, straight up. The center of the rope caught on a piece of the sky so that both ends of the rope hung down to the rock.

The women tied all their own ropes to the ends of the rope hanging from the sky. Then they clasped hands and called:

"Eagle-down ropes, magic ropes, help us!"

They stood on the ropes which were spread on the rock and began to sing to the magic ropes, with a special magic song.

Then, because they knew so much magic and had magic ropes, the ropes slowly began to rise and swing around and around the way Buzzard flies.

As the wives sang louder the ropes made bigger and bigger circles in the sky.

Soon the women standing on the ropes were sailing through the sky over the village where they lived.

Their fathers and mothers looked up and saw them in the sky. People of the village pointed up at them and were very excited.

The women in the sky saw their mothers and fathers and their mothers-in-law and fathers-in-law rush into huts. Next they saw them come out with mush and beads and belts and put all these things on the ground.

"Come back!" the women's relatives cried up at them. "Come back and see what we have for you!"

But the women just stayed in the sky.

Down below, the husbands looked up and saw their wives. "Why didn't you keep an eye on them?" they scolded their

31

wives' parents. "Why did you let them get away when we were out hunting?"

Now that the wives were gone, the husbands wanted them back. They were lonesome and sad. They got together and tried to think what to do.

They decided to use their own magic eagle-down ropes and go up in the sky after their wives.

They climbed the rock, put down their ropes and sang in the same way their wives had done. Soon they were sailing in the sky over the village.

Old people came out and begged their sons to come back, but the sons wanted their wives, so they kept on singing and going higher and higher into the sky.

By this time the wives were very high in the sky because they had a head start on the husbands. They looked down and saw their husbands coming after them.

"Shall we let them catch us?" they asked each other.

"No!" said one. "Our husbands said they didn't want us any more. Don't let them catch up with us, ever."

All agreed they would rather be alone in the sky.

As soon as the husbands got close enough, the women shouted down. "Stay where you are!"

The wives had stronger magic in their eagle-down ropes and their magic song. The men had to stay right where they were—below their wives.

They all turned into stars where they are to this day.

White people call the higher group of six stars the Pleiades. Indians call them the Young Women. The lower set of six stars, white people call Taurus. Indians call them the Young Men.

Whatever the name, there they are, swinging slowly across the sky on clear nights—and all because the Mono Indian women loved to eat wild onions more than anything else.

Anne Fisher retells this tale in *Stories California Indians Told* (1957). Many Native American tales are mythic stories which explain the natural world. Native Americans in different parts of the country have different stories to explain how the constellations appeared.

KATE CRACKERNUTS

Once upon a time, far to the north of Scotland, there lived a king and a queen. The king had a daughter, Anne, and the noblewoman he married had a daughter named Kate. The two girls grew to love each other dearly.

However, after a time the new queen became jealous of Anne, thinking her bonnier than her own daughter Kate. It was a foolish notion for the two girls were both fine lasses, one fair-haired, one dark-haired. Nonetheless the foolish queen said to herself, "Should a prince come riding by, Anne will surely marry him; and her father would settle the kingdom on the pair, no doubt!"

This fretted her mind sorely till at last she went to consult a local henwife who was known for her magic potions and spells. The henwife took the queen's gold piece and told her she knew a magic spell that would suit her purpose. "Send the lassie to me early in the morn," she said, "but be sure 'tis before she's had food or drink."

So early the next morning the queen said to Anne, "Go, my dear, to the henwife in the glen and ask her for fresh eggs." Anne set out, but as she passed through the kitchen, she saw a crust of bread. Being quite hungry, she took it and munched it as she went along.

When she reached the cottage Anne said, "The queen has sent me for fresh eggs."

"Come in, lass," said the henwife. "Now lift the lid of that pot and see what you'll see!" Anne did this, but nothing happened.

The henwife said crossly, "Go home to the queen and tell her to keep her larder door better locked!"

Anne took the eggs and went home to the queen to tell her what the henwife had said. The queen knew from this that Anne had had something to eat, so she watched carefully the next morning and sent Anne away fasting. But the princess saw some country folk picking peas by the roadside, and being a friendly lass, she stopped to talk with them. They offered her a handful of fresh peas, and these she took to eat on the way.

When she told the henwife she had come for eggs, the henwife said, "Lift the lid off that pot and see what you'll see!" Anne lifted the lid and peered in, but still nothing happened. Then the henwife was rare angry and said, "Tell the queen the pot won't boil if the fire's away." Anne went home and told this to the queen.

The third day the queen went along with Anne to the henwife to make sure Anne had neither food nor drink. Now this time, when Anne lifted the lid off the pot to peer inside, her bonny head was suddenly turned into a sheep's head. The queen was dismayed. She had not intended anything so drastic to happen to Anne.

How the maids in the castle stared and tittered when they saw Anne! As for Kate, she said she would bide at home no longer. She would go out into the world to seek her fortune and take her sister Anne with her. So she wrapped a fine linen kerchief about her sister's face and head and off they went with a bannock* to eat on the way.

They walked on and on, over a mountain and down the other side, till at last they came to a castle. Kate knocked at the door and asked a night's lodging for herself and her sick sister.

The two sisters were fed and given a room, but they were not long in the castle before Kate saw something was amiss.

*A bannock is a round bread made of oatmeal or barley.

Such lamenting and grieving among the castle folk! She learned the young prince had a strange illness and no one could discover what ailed him. He lay abed, pale and weak, sleeping so heavily all the day that no one could rouse him. The king was fair beside himself with worry, and he had offered a peck of gold to anyone who could restore the prince to health. But the curious thing, the castle folk told Kate, was that anyone who sat up all night with the prince was never seen again.

"A peck of gold is a fine fortune," Kate said to Anne. "With that we could seek out a way to break the wicked spell on you." So Kate went to the king and said she would try to discover what ailed the prince.

The king shook his head in doubt. "It's a strange matter surely. All manner of herb remedies and word charms have been tried, and doctors brought in." Reluctantly, he gave orders for Kate to be brought to the prince's chamber.

When Kate saw the pale young prince sleeping so heavily, she felt a great pity for him. She was a brave girl, and she was determined she would sit up with him through the night to see what she could see.

That night the prince slept on, and Kate sat in a chair before the fire. All was quiet in the castle until midnight. Then suddenly up rose the sick prince from his bed, dressed himself, and went down the stairs. His eyes were open, but he did not notice Kate. He seemed like one asleep or entranced. Kate followed him quietly.

The prince went to the stable where he saddled and mounted his horse. Kate leapt lightly up behind him. Away rode the prince and Kate through the greenwood. The moon shone faintly through the trees, and Kate saw the branches on either side of them were heavy with hazel nuts. She plucked the nuts as they passed, filling both her pockets with them.

They rode on and on until at last they came to a green hill, a high, grass-covered mound. Here the prince drew rein and called, "Open! Open green hill and let the young prince in." "And the lady behind him," added Kate.

The green hill opened, and the prince dismounted. Kate quickly slid off the horse and hid in the shadows near the entrance. The prince entered a magnificent great hall brilliantly lit as though by thousands of candles. But candles there were none—it was the light given off by all the fairy host gathered there. Fair, shimmering fairy women surrounded the prince and led him off to the dance. The prince danced on and on to the fairy music till he could dance no longer and fell upon a couch. Then the fairy women would fan him for a few minutes and bring him right back into the dance.

At last the cock crowed, and Kate slipped outside the fairy hill. The prince made haste to leave the great hall. The hill closed behind them, and the prince climbed wearily onto his horse. Kate mounted behind him, and home they rode.

When the castle servants came into the prince's chamber in the morning, they found the prince heavily asleep in his bed and Kate beside the fire cracking the nuts she had gathered. But naught did she say of what had happened in the night until she went back to her sister's chamber. Then Kate told her sister of the fairy hill. She had found the cause of the prince's strange sickness, but she knew no way to break the fairies' spell.

Anne became very alarmed, and begged Kate not to follow the prince through the greenwood again. "If the fairies discover you there, they will be angry—they will keep you under that fairy hill for seven years!" But Kate said she must go if the prince again rode off at night.

The second night passed in the same way. The prince rose at midnight and rode off to the fairy hill, Kate astride behind him. Again she gathered nuts from the trees and filled her pockets. This time after the prince had entered the great hall, Kate crept a little closer to watch and listen. She could hear the fairy women speak to each other, and she saw a small fairy child playing nearby. Again the prince whirled and leapt and danced to the fairy music.

"The bonny prince will not last much longer in the outer world," said one fairy woman as she danced past. "Then he will be with us forever!" Kate felt despair when she heard this. She turned away from the merry dancers to watch the fairy child, hardly more than a babe, playing with a small polished stick the shape of a shepherd's crook. She heard one fairy woman say, "The babe should not be playing with the rowan wand." But the other shrugged and answered, "No matter. 'Tis only a charm against sheep's head spells." The fairies danced on.

Kate knew she must have that rowan crook, so she rolled some of the nuts from her pocket till the babe dropped the stick and went after the nuts. Kate quickly reached out for the crook and put it into her pocket.

At cockcrow they rode home as before. Kate hurried to her sister's room and touched Anne's head three times with the rowan crook. The dreadful sheep's head disappeared, and Anne was once more her own bonny self!

But the prince still lay abed, heavily asleep, paler and thinner than ever. Kate said she would sit up with the prince one more night.

At midnight on the third night the prince rose as before. Kate followed him, leapt onto the horse behind him, and together they rode through the greenwood. Once more she plucked the nuts from the branches as they passed and filled her pockets.

Once more the prince danced and whirled in the fairy hill, while Kate, hidden close by the entrance, watched and listened to all that was said. This night a fairy child was playing nearby with a small willow basket, and Kate heard one woman say, "'Tis not wise to let the child have that with the prince here." But the other laughed and said, "The prince doesn't know that to eat of that bird would break our spell!"

Kate rolled out her nuts, one after another, until the basket was dropped, and the child followed the nuts. Kate quickly reached out for the little basket and put it into her pocket.

At cockcrow they returned home to the castle. The prince undressed and fell into bed. Kate undid the latch and opened the basket. She took out the strange bird, plucked the feathers, and cooked the bird over the fire. Soon a savory smell filled the room.

The prince awoke and cried out, "Oh, I wish I had a bite of that bird!"

So Kate gave him a bite, and he rose up on one elbow. Kate gave him a second bite, and he sat up on his bed. Then he said, "If I had but a third bite of that bird. . .!" So Kate gave him a third bite, and he stood up hale and strong.

He dressed himself and sat down by the hearth. When the castle folk came in the next morning, they found Kate and the young prince cracking nuts together and roasting them over the fire.

Great was the feasting and celebration on the young prince's recovery! And you may be sure that Kate and Anne, as honored guests, joined in dancing and games right merrily. The folk in the Orkney Islands still tell of it, for the feasting and the drinking and the merrymaking went on for seven weeks. And they say that all who were there "lived happy, died happy, and never drank out of a dry cappy."*

The original and only version of this tale was collected in the nineteenth century from an elderly woman in the Orkney Islands off the north coast of Scotland.

*A cappy is a cup.

THREE STRONG WOMEN

Long ago, in Japan, there lived a famous wrestler, and he was on his way to the capital city to wrestle before the Emperor.

He strode down the road on legs thick as the trunks of small trees. He had been walking for seven hours and could, and probably would, walk for seven more without getting tired.

The time was autumn, the sky was a cold, watery blue, the air chilly. In the small bright sun, the trees along the roadside glowed red and orange.

The wrestler hummed to himself, "Zun-zun-zun," in time with the long swing of his legs. Wind blew through his thin brown robe, and he wore no sword at his side. He felt proud that he needed no sword, even in the darkest and loneliest places. The icy air on his body only reminded him that few tailors would have been able to make expensive warm clothes for a man so broad and tall. He felt much as a wrestler should—strong, healthy, and rather conceited.

A soft roar of fast-moving water beyond the trees told him that he was passing above a river bank. He "zun-zunned" louder; he loved the sound of his voice and wanted it to sound clearly above the rushing water.

He thought: They call me Forever-Mountain because I am such a good strong wrestler—big, too. I'm a fine, brave man and far too modest ever to say so. . . .

Just then he saw a girl who must have come up from the river, for she steadied a bucket on her head.

Her hands on the bucket were small, and there was a dimple on each thumb, just below the knuckle. She was a round girl with red cheeks and a nose like a friendly button. Her eyes looked as though she were thinking of ten thousand funny stories at once. She clambered up onto the road and walked ahead of the wrestler, jolly and bounceful.

"If I don't tickle that fat girl, I shall regret it all my life," said the wrestler under his breath. "She's sure to go 'squeak' and I shall laugh and laugh. If she drops her bucket, that will be even funnier—and I can always run and fill it again and even carry it home for her."

He tiptoed up and poked her lightly in the ribs with one huge finger.

"Kochokochokocho!" he said, a fine, ticklish sound in Japanese.

The girl gave a satisfying squeal, giggled, and brought one arm down so that the wrestler's hand was caught between it and her body.

"Ho-ho-ho! You've caught me! I can't move at all!" said the wrestler, laughing.

"I know," said the jolly girl.

He felt that it was very good-tempered of her to take a joke so well, and started to pull his hand free.

Somehow, he could not.

He tried again, using a little more strength.

"Now, now—let me go," he said. "I am a very powerful man. If I pull too hard I might hurt you."

"Pull," said the girl. "I admire powerful men."

She began to walk, and though the wrestler tugged and pulled until his feet dug great furrows in the ground, he had to follow. She couldn't have paid him less attention if he had been a puppy—a small one.

Ten minutes later, still tugging while trudging helplessly after her, he was glad that the road was lonely and no one was there to see.

"Please let me go," he pleaded. "I am the famous wrestler Forever-Mountain. I must go and show my strength before the

40

Emperor"—he burst out weeping from shame and confusion—
"and you're hurting my hand!"

The girl steadied the bucket on her head with her free
hand and dimpled sympathetically over her shoulder. "You
poor, sweet little Forever-Mountain," she said. "Are you tired?
Shall I carry you? I can leave the water here and come back for
it later."

"I do not want you to carry me. I want you to let me go,
and then I want to forget I ever saw you. What do you want with
me?" moaned the pitiful wrestler.

"I only want to help you," said the girl, now pulling him
steadily up and up a narrow mountain path. "Oh, I am sure
you'll have no more trouble than anyone else when you come
up against the other wrestlers. You'll win, or else you'll lose,
and you won't be too badly hurt either way. But aren't you
afraid you might meet a really strong man someday?"

Forever-Mountain turned white. He stumbled. He was
imagining being laughed at throughout Japan as "Hardly-Ever-
Mountain."

She glanced back.

"You see? Tired already," she said. "I'll walk more slowly.
Why don't you come along to my mother's house and let us
make a strong man of you? The wrestling in the capital isn't
due to begin for three months. I know, because Grandmother
thought she'd go. You'd be spending all that time in bad company and wasting what little power you have."

"All right. Three months. I'll come along," said the wrestler. He felt he had nothing more to lose. Also, he feared that
the girl might become angry if he refused, and place him in the
top of a tree until he changed his mind.

"Fine," she said happily. "We are almost there."

She freed his hand. It had become red and a little swollen.
"But if you break your promise and run off, I shall have to
chase you and carry you back."

Soon they arrived in a small valley. A simple farmhouse
with a thatched roof stood in the middle.

"Grandmother is at home, but she is an old lady and she's

probably sleeping." The girl shaded her eyes with one hand. "But Mother should be bringing our cow back from the field—oh, there's Mother now!"

She waved. The woman coming around the corner of the house put down the cow she was carrying and waved back.

She smiled and came across the grass, walking with a lively bounce like her daughter's. Well, maybe her bounce was a little more solid, thought the wrestler.

"Excuse me," she said, brushing some cow hair from her dress and dimpling, also like her daughter. "These mountain paths are full of stones. They hurt the cow's feet. And who is the nice young man you've brought, Maru-me?"

The girl explained. "And we have only three months!" she finished anxiously.

"Well, it's not long enough to do much, but it's not so short a time we can't do something," said her mother, looking thoughtful. "But he does look terribly feeble. He'll need a lot of good things to eat. Maybe when he gets stronger he can help Grandmother with some of the easy work about the house."

"That will be fine!" said the girl, and she called her grandmother—loudly, for the old lady was a little deaf.

"I'm coming!" came a creaky voice from inside the house, and a little old woman leaning on a stick and looking very sleepy tottered out of the door. As she came toward them she stumbled over the roots of a great oak tree.

"Heh! My eyes aren't what they used to be. That's the fourth time this month I've stumbled over that tree," she complained and, wrapping her skinny arms about its trunk, pulled it out of the ground.

"Oh, Grandmother! You should have let me pull it up for you," said Maru-me.

"Hm. I hope I didn't hurt my poor old back," muttered the old lady. She called out, "Daughter! Throw that tree away like a good girl, so no one will fall over it. But make sure it doesn't hit anybody."

"You can help Mother with the tree," Maru-me said to

*Maru-me began to walk and, though the wrestler
tugged and pulled, he had to follow.*

Forever-Mountain. "On second thought, you'd better not help. Just watch."

Her mother went to the tree, picked it up in her two hands, and threw it. Up went the tree, sailing end over end, growing smaller and smaller as it flew. It landed with a faint crash far up the mountainside.

"Ah, how clumsy," she said. "I meant to throw it over the mountain. It's probably blocking the path now, and I'll have to get up early tomorrow to move it."

The wrestler was not listening. He had very quietly fainted.

"Oh! We must put him to bed," said Maru-me.

"Poor, feeble young man," said her mother.

"I hope we can do something for him. Here, let me carry him, he's light," said the grandmother. She slung him over her shoulder and carried him into the house, creaking along with her cane.

The next day they began the work of making Forever-Mountain over into what they thought a strong man should be. They gave him the simplest food to eat, and the toughest. Day by day they prepared his rice with less and less water, until no ordinary man could have chewed or digested it.

Every day he was made to do the work of five men, and every evening he wrestled with Grandmother. Maru-me and her mother agreed that Grandmother, being old and feeble, was the least likely to injure him accidentally. They hoped the exercise might be good for the old lady's rheumatism.

He grew stronger and stronger but was hardly aware of it. Grandmother could still throw him easily into the air—and catch him again—without ever changing her sweet old smile.

He quite forgot that outside this valley he was one of the greatest wrestlers in Japan and was called Forever-Mountain. His legs had been like logs; now they were like pillars. His big hands were hard as stones, and when he cracked his knuckles the sound was like trees splitting on a cold night.

Sometimes he did an exercise that wrestlers do in Japan— raising one foot high above the ground and bringing it down with a crash. Then people in nearby villages looked up at the winter sky and told one another that it was very late in the year for thunder.

Soon he could pull up a tree as well as the grandmother. He could even throw one—but only a small distance. One evening, near the end of his third month, he wrestled with Grandmother and held her down for half a minute.

"Heh-heh!" She chortled and got up, smiling with every wrinkle. "I would never have believed it!"

Maru-me squealed with joy and threw her arms around him—gently, for she was afraid of cracking his ribs.

"Very good, very good! What a strong man," said her mother, who had just come home from the fields, carrying, as usual, the cow. She put the cow down and patted the wrestler on the back.

They agreed that he was now ready to show some real strength before the Emperor.

"Take the cow along with you tomorrow when you go," said the mother. "Sell her and buy yourself a belt—a silken belt. Buy the fattest and heaviest one you can find. Wear it when you appear before the Emperor, as a souvenir from us."

"I wouldn't think of taking your only cow. You've already done too much for me. And you'll need her to plow the fields, won't you?"

They burst out laughing. Maru-me squealed, her mother roared. The grandmother cackled so hard and long that she choked and had to be pounded on the back.

"Oh, dear," said the mother, still laughing. "You didn't think we used our cow for anything like work! Why, Grandmother here is stronger than five cows!"

"The cow is our pet." Maru-me giggled. "She has lovely brown eyes."

"But it really gets tiresome having to carry her back and forth each day so that she has enough grass to eat," said her mother.

"Then you must let me give you all the prize money that I win," said Forever-Mountain.

45

"Oh, no! We wouldn't think of it!" said Maru-me. "Because we all like you too much to sell you anything. And it is not proper to accept gifts of money from strangers."

"True," said Forever-Mountain. "I will now ask your mother's and grandmother's permission to marry you. I want to be one of the family."

"Oh! I'll get a wedding dress ready!" said Maru-me.

The mother and grandmother pretended to consider very seriously, but they quickly agreed.

Next morning Forever-Mountain tied his hair up in the topknot that all Japanese wrestlers wear, and got ready to leave. He thanked Maru-me and her mother and bowed very low to the grandmother, since she was the oldest and had been a fine wrestling partner.

Then he picked up the cow in his arms and trudged up the mountain. When he reached the top, he slung the cow over one shoulder and waved good-by to Maru-me.

At the first town he came to, Forever-Mountain sold the cow. She brought a good price because she was unusually fat from never having worked in her life. With the money, he bought the heaviest silken belt he could find.

When he reached the palace grounds, many of the other wrestlers were already there, sitting about, eating enormous bowls of rice, comparing one another's weight and telling stories. They paid little attention to Forever-Mountain except to wonder why he had arrived so late this year. Some of them noticed that he had grown very quiet and took no part at all in their boasting.

All the ladies and gentlemen of the court were waiting in a special courtyard for the wrestling to begin. They wore many robes, one on top of another, heavy with embroidery and gold cloth, and sweat ran down their faces and froze in the winter af-ternoon. The gentlemen had long swords so weighted with gold and precious stones that they could never have used them, even if they had known how. The court ladies, with their long black hair hanging down behind, had their faces painted dead white, which made them look frightened. They had pulled out their real eyebrows and painted new ones high above the place where eyebrows are supposed to be, and this made them all look as though they were very surprised at something.

Behind a screen sat the Emperor—by himself, because he was too noble for ordinary people to look at. He was a lonely old man with a kind, tired face. He hoped the wrestling would end quickly so that he could go to his room and write poems.

The first two wrestlers chosen to fight were Forever-Mountain and a wrestler who was said to have the biggest stomach in the country. He and Forever-Mountain both threw some salt into the ring. It was understood that this drove away evil spirits.

Then the other wrestler, moving his stomach somewhat out of the way, raised his foot and brought it down with a fearful stamp. He glared fiercely at Forever-Mountain as if to say, "Now you stamp, you poor frightened man!"

Forever-Mountain raised his foot. He brought it down.

There was a sound like thunder, the earth shook, and the other wrestler bounced into the air and out of the ring, as gracefully as any soap bubble.

He picked himself up and bowed to the Emperor's screen.

"The earth-god is angry. Possibly there is something the matter with the salt," he said. "I do not think I shall wrestle this season." And he walked out, looking very suspiciously over one shoulder at Forever-Mountain.

Five other wrestlers then and there decided that they were not wrestling this season, either. They all looked annoyed with Forever-Mountain.

From then on, Forever-Mountain brought his foot down lightly. As each wrestler came into the ring, he picked him up very gently, carried him out, and placed him before the Emperor's screen, bowing most courteously every time.

The court ladies' eyebrows went up even higher. The gentlemen looked disturbed and a little afraid. They loved to see fierce, strong men tugging and grunting at each other, but Forever-Mountain was a little too much for them. Only the Emperor was happy behind his screen, for now, with the wrestling over so quickly, he would have that much more time to write his poems. He ordered all the prize money handed over to Forever-Mountain.

"But," he said, "you had better not wrestle any more." He stuck a finger through his screen and waggled it at the other wrestlers, who were sitting on the ground weeping with disappointment like great fat babies.

Forever-Mountain promised not to wrestle any more. Everybody looked relieved. The wrestlers sitting on the ground almost smiled.

"I think I shall become a farmer," Forever-Mountain said, and left at once to go back to Maru-me.

Maru-me was waiting for him. When she saw him coming, she ran down the mountain, picked him up, together with the heavy bags of prize money, and carried him halfway up the mountainside. Then she giggled and put him down. The rest of the way she let him carry her.

Forever-Mountain kept his promise to the Emperor and never fought in public again. His name was forgotten in the capital. But up in the mountains, sometimes, the earth shakes and rumbles, and they say that is Forever-Mountain and Maru-me's grandmother practicing wrestling in the hidden valley.

According to the author Claus Stamm, this folk tale is still told in Japan. Stamm's version of the tall story reprinted here originally appeared in 1962.

THE BLACK BULL OF NORROWAY

Long ago in Norroway there lived a woman who had three daughters. Off they went one day to learn their fortunes from an old woman who lived in the forest. The oldest daughter was told she would marry an earl, the second daughter that she would marry a lord, and the youngest—a black bull.

The two older sisters were very pleased with their fortunes, but the youngest sister laughed and said, "No matter, I'll be content with the Black Bull of Norroway!"

Her sisters warned her not to jest of such a monster, lest it become true.

"I'm not so eager to marry," she declared. "I'll stay at home until the Black Bull comes to court me.

Well, the two older sisters went out into the world, and one did marry an earl, and the other did marry a lord. Nonetheless, the youngest sister was quite surprised one day to see a great big black bull at the door. At first the girl was afraid, but the bull seemed gentle and quiet. He looked at her with steady eyes and said he'd come to fetch her.

"I promised I would be content with the Black Bull of Norroway," she said to her mother, "and I will keep my word." So she climbed onto his back and off they went. And always the Bull chose the smoothest paths, the easiest roads, and was careful not to brush against thorns and briers.

On they rode until the girl was almost faint with hunger. The Black Bull said to her in a soft, friendly voice, "Reach into my right ear, and you will find food. Reach into my left ear, and you will find drink." She did so, and after drinking and eating, she gathered the remains in her kerchief to eat later.

Toward evening they came in sight of a fine castle. "Yonder lives my eldest brother," said the Black Bull, "and there we must stay tonight."

When they arrived at the castle the girl was made welcome, and the Black Bull was sent out to the fields with others of his kind. The next morning before she took her leave, she was given a golden walnut by the people in the castle. They told her not to break it open until she was in the worst trouble ever a person could be, and then it would help her.

She climbed onto the back of the Black Bull, and they traveled on through forests and over mountains. From the Black Bull's right ear she had food, and from his left ear she had drink. On the way they talked with each other, and the girl found him a cheerful companion.

When evening drew near, they came in sight of a castle grander than the first one. The Black Bull said, "Yonder my second brother lives, and there we must stay this night." The girl was made welcome by the people of the castle, and this time she asked that the Black Bull be fed well and stabled, for she had become very fond of him.

The next morning, before they set off again, she was given a large golden hickory nut by the castle folk. They told her not to use it until she was in the worst trouble in the world, and it would bring her through it. Again the Black Bull magically provided food and drink, and they talked as they traveled on. That evening they reached a very grand castle. "Yonder lives my youngest brother," said the Bull, "and here we must stay the night."

The girl was made welcome at the castle. But she would not leave the Black Bull until she made sure he was brushed and fed, and settled comfortably in the stable. The next morning she was given a large golden hazelnut by the castle folk. Again she was told not to open it until she was in the worst straits ever, and then it would help her.

Now they rode on and on until they reached a dark and ugsome glen. The Black Bull told her that the time had come for him to try to break his enchantment. The Bull halted, and she slid down from his back.

"Here you must stay while I go on and fight the Old One," said the Bull. "He is powerful, and I do not know what monstrous shape he will be. If I destroy him, the trolls' enchantment will be broken, and I will be once more a man."

The Black Bull then led her to a great rock. "There is one thing you must do. You must sit on this rock and move neither hand nor foot while I'm gone—or I shall never find you again. And if everything round about you turns blue, it means I have beaten the creature; but if all things turn red, he will have conquered me." And with a loud bellow, the Black Bull set out to find his foe.

The girl sat upon the rock, still as could be, moving neither hand nor foot. She waited and waited and waited; then all around her turned blue. In the far distance, through the eerie blue light, she glimpsed the tall and bloodstained figure of a knight. Overcome with joy at her friend's victory, she moved her foot.

Long she waited, but he did not return for the enchantment was but partly broken. And though he searched for her in the glen, he could not find her.

Then she wept, for she knew that by moving her foot, she had failed to help him break the enchantment; he was still under the power of the trolls. She touched the three golden nuts in her pocket, but the time had not yet come to use them. She would search for him and free him if she could.

Wearily she got up and walked on and on for many days, till she came to a great hill of glass. Round the bottom of the hill she went, trying to climb it; but she could not.

At last she came to a smith's forge. The smith promised

he would make her iron shoes to climb the hill of glass, if she would work for him for seven months and seven days. She worked in the forge the seven months and seven days, and the smith gave her the iron shoes. He warned her the glass hill led to the country of the trolls, but she paid him no mind and climbed the hill.

When she reached the land of the trolls, she heard talk of a gallant knight who was forced to dwell among them. They were determined the knight should marry one of the troll women, but he had refused even the troll princess. He had said he could marry no one until the blood was washed from his clothes.

It was proclaimed that whoever could wash the knight's garments clean should be his bride. There was a great clatter as one troll woman after another tried to wash the torn, blood-stained garments. Their hairy bodies glistened and their red eyes gleamed as they scrubbed and washed, but the blood stains would not come out.

When the troll princess saw the strange girl who had come into their land, she set her to work washing the knight's bloody garments. When the girl washed the clothes, the stains came out at once, leaving the garments pure and clean. But the troll princess brought the garments to the captive knight and claimed that she herself had washed them clean, and that she would marry him.

Now the girl was in despair. The marriage was to be held the next day. How could she save him? Surely this was the time to open the golden walnut! She broke it open and found it was full of precious jewels.

She knew all trolls are greedy, so she brought them to the troll princess and said, "All these I will give you if you put off the wedding one day and let me go into the bridegroom's chamber alone at night."

The troll princess agreed, but she gave the young knight a sleeping potion in the evening.

When the girl went into the room of her beloved, he was sleeping heavily, and she could not wake him. She spoke to him, called to him, and sang to him:

> The smith's forge I worked for thee,
> The glassy hill I climbed for thee,
> Thy bloody clothes I wrung for thee;
> Will thou not waken and turn to me?

But he slept on and did not waken. When dawn came, the girl left, and he never knew she had been there.

The next day her heart was full of grief. She broke open the golden hickory nut, and the jewels inside were more brilliant than the others. So again she offered the rich jewels to the greedy troll princess, if she would put off the wedding one more day and allow her to stay the night in the room where the young man slept. But again the troll princess gave the knight a sleeping potion.

Again the girl tried to wake him. She called to him and she sang to him:

> The smith's forge I worked for thee,
> The glassy hill I climbed for thee,
> Thy bloody clothes I wrung for thee;
> Will thou not waken and turn to me?

But he slept heavily until morning and never knew she had been there.

The girl felt her heart would break. She had only the hazelnut left, so she opened it, and inside were the most brilliant jewels of all. When she showed these jewels to the troll princess, the princess could not resist them. She agreed to allow the girl in the room one last night.

Now it happened that the same day, the young man overheard two troll servants talking together about the strange sighs and singing in the captive knight's chamber. The young man resolved to stay awake that night to see who came into his room. He suspected that the posset he was given to drink that evening was a sleeping potion, and he secretly poured it away.

This time the girl found the young knight wide awake when she entered his room. He recognized her at once, and as

soon as they embraced each other, the trolls' spell was broken
—finally and completely.

While all around them slept, they silently left the house
and hurried away from the land of the trolls. They slid down the
glass hill and made their way back to their own country.

And there, in a fine castle of their own, they lived in peace
and contentment ever after.

Different versions of this tale exist in England. It has Norse elements—the eerie
blue light, the glass hill—and is believed to be very old. This retelling by the
editor uses Joseph Jacobs and Florie Annie Steele as sources.

KAMALA AND THE
SEVEN THIEVES

In a Punjabi* village long ago, there lived a woman named Kamala. Her husband, a barber, was a cheerful fellow who would much rather sit in the dusty square and gossip than practice his trade. So of course they became poorer and poorer, until one day there was not a penny in the house for food.

"Business has been very slow," said the barber. "Even the traders in the market say so."

"That may be," answered Kamala, "but I don't intend to starve. The Rajah is holding a great wedding feast at the Palace. You must go to him and ask for something. It would be bad luck to refuse you on such an occasion."

The barber sighed, but off he went to the palace. When he was brought before the Rajah to make his plea, he was too dazzled by the brilliant silks, and the sparkling jewels, and the huge feathered fans moving to and fro, to think very clearly. The thought of food or alms simply flew out of his mind.

"Speak up!" snapped the Wazir.

The poor barber stammered that he hoped the Rajah "would give him something."

"Something?" said the Rajah impatiently. "What thing?"

"Anything, anything you don't need," blurted the barber.

"Give him a piece of wasteland near his village," ordered the Rajah. This was done, and the barber went home quite relieved that the ordeal was over.

*Punjabi is now West Pakistan.

55

"Wasteland!" exclaimed Kamala who had had her cooking pots cleaned and ready. "And how will I cook that for our dinner?"

"Land is land," said the barber solemnly.

"So it is—but what good is wasteland unless we till it? Where are we to get bullocks and plow? Or seed?"

The barber could give no answer. So, being a resourceful woman, Kamala sat down to think of a plan to make the best of their situation.

The next day she took her husband with her and set off for the piece of wasteland. Telling her husband to imitate her, she began walking about the field peering anxiously at the ground and poking it here and there with a sharp stick. When anyone came that way, they would sit down and pretend to be doing nothing at all.

This strange behavior caught the attention of two thieves passing by. They immediately summoned the rest of the gang and all seven of them hid in the bushes nearby. They watched the couple all day, for they were convinced that something mysterious was going on. After arguing about it endlessly, one of the thieves was sent to find out.

Kamala pretended to be evasive, but finally she said, "It is a family secret. You must promise not to tell a soul." Of course the thief eagerly promised to keep the secret.

"The fact is," said Kamala solemnly, "we've just learned this field of ours has five pots full of gold buried in it. We were just trying to discover the exact spot before beginning to dig tomorrow."

With that Kamala and her husband returned home, and the thief ran to his companions to tell them of the hidden treasure. The seven thieves set to work at once. All night long they dug and turned over the earth in a perfect frenzy, until the field looked as if it had been plowed seven times over; but not a gold piece—or even a penny—did they find. When dawn came, they went away tired and disgusted, grumbling over their blistered hands.

The next day when Kamala found the field so well plowed, she was delighted at the success of her plan. She hurried to the grain dealer's shop and borrowed rice to sow in the field, promising to pay it back with interest at harvest time. And so she did, for never was there such a fine crop! Kamala paid her debts, kept some rice for the house, and sold the rest for enough gold pieces to fill a large earthen crock.

When the thieves saw this, they were very angry indeed. They hastened to the barber's hut and confronted Kamala.

"Give us a share of the harvest money," they demanded brazenly. "We dug up the ground for you. You can't deny that."

Kamala simply laughed at them. "I told you there was gold in the ground! You tried to find it to steal it, didn't you? But I knew how to get gold from the earth, and you rascals shan't have a penny of it!"

"If you won't give us a share of it, we'll take it!"

"You'll have to find it first!" Kamala retorted and slammed the door on them.

Nonetheless, she kept a sharp lookout, and that evening she noticed one of the thieves had crept up to the house and hidden himself under the open window.

"What have you done with the gold, my dear?" asked the barber. "I hope you haven't put it under our pillows!"

"Don't be alarmed," she said in a loud voice, "the gold is not in the house. I have hung it in the branches of the nim tree outside. No one will think of looking for it there."

The thief outside the window heard this, as he was meant to, and he hurried off chuckling to tell his companions. When everyone had gone to sleep, the band of thieves gathered under the tree.

"There it is!" cried the captain of the band, peering up into the branches. "One of you go up and bring it down." Now what he saw was really a hornets' nest full of great brown and yellow hornets, but in the faint moonlight it looked like a bag of gold.

So one of the thieves climbed up the tree. But when he came close and was just reaching up to take hold of it, a hornet flew out and stung him on the thigh, causing him to clap his hand to the spot.

The watchers below cried out angrily, "He's taking gold pieces for himself! He's put one in his pocket!"

"I am not," retorted the thief. "Something bit me!" But just at that moment another hornet stung him on the breast, and he smacked his hand there.

"We saw you!" cried the thieves below, and they sent up another man to bring down the gold. But he fared no better for the hornets were by now thoroughly aroused, and he, too, began to smack his hands about him. The other thieves danced with rage, convinced he was also pocketing gold pieces.

"They're stealing our gold!" bawled the thieves below, and one after another they climbed up into the tree, eager to get their share of the loot. As soon as they reached the branch nearest the hornets' nest, they all began slapping their clothes as if they were filling their pockets.

The angry leader of the band climbed up last. Determined to have the prize, he seized hold of the hornets' nest. At that moment the branch they were all standing on broke, and they all came tumbling to the ground with the hornets' nest on top of them. What a stampede there was! They scrambled off in all directions with the buzzing hornets in pursuit.

After that Kamala and her husband saw nothing of the thieves for quite a while. They were all laid up with injuries, and the couple was very pleased to be rid of them.

"They don't dare to come back!" said Kamala to her husband. But she was wrong. The gang of thieves was planning its revenge.

One night when it was very hot, the barber and his wife put their beds outside to sleep. The thieves, seizing their chance, lifted up Kamala's bed and carried her off fast asleep. She woke to find herself borne along on the heads of four of the thieves, while the other three ran along beside. She gave herself up for lost; there did not seem any way to escape.

Then the robbers paused for breath under a large tree.

Quick as a wink she seized hold of a branch and swung herself into the tree, leaving the quilt on the bed just as if she were still in it.

"Let us rest here awhile," said the men carrying the bed. "There's plenty of time, and we're tired. She's dreadfully heavy!" And they set their burden down to one side.

Kamala kept very still, for it was a bright moonlit night. The thieves argued over who should first stand guard while the others slept. It fell to the leader, so he walked up and down as guard. Meanwhile, Kamala sat perched up in the tree like a great bird.

Suddenly she had an idea, and drawing the thin white material of her garment over her face, she began to sing softly.

When the leader looked up and saw the veiled figure of a woman in the tree he was, of course, surprised. But being a young fellow and quite vain about his looks, he at once decided it must be a fairy or peri who had fallen in love with his handsome face. He had heard of such happenings, especially on moonlit nights. So he twirled his moustaches and strutted about, waiting for her to speak.

But when she went on singing and took no notice of him, he stopped and called out, "Come down, my beauty! I won't hurt you!"

Still she went on singing. So he climbed into the tree, smoothing his hair and patting his moustache as he went. When he came quite close, she turned her head away and uttered a long mournful sigh.

"What is the matter, my little one?" he asked tenderly. "You are a fairy and you have fallen in love with me, but why should you sigh so sadly?"

"Aaah," sighed Kamala again. "I believe you are fickle! You will soon forget me!"

"Never!" cried the leader of the thieves.

"Take a bite of this fairy fruit, and then I shall know if you are sincere." As she said this, she plucked a large pomegranate from the tree and rammed it into the thief's open mouth.

Startled, the thief tumbled off the branch and crashed to the ground where he sat with his legs wide apart, looking as if he'd fallen from the sky.

"What is the matter?" cried his comrades awakened by the noise.

"Ah—aagh—aagh" was all he could say as he pointed up into the tree, for his mouth was firmly gagged with the fruit, and he was too stunned to know what had happened.

"The man is bewitched," cried one. "There must be a ghost in the tree!"

Just then Kamala began flapping her veil and howling eerily. Whoooeeewhoooeeee! The thieves were terrified. They ran off as fast as they could, dragging their leader behind them.

When they were over the hill and out of sight, Kamala came down from the tree, balanced her cot on top of her head, and walked home.

And that was the end of the attempt to steal the gold—for the robbers didn't stop running until they reached the next village and they never came back.

Tales from the Punjab area of India, now part of West Pakistan, are known for their humor. This is a retelling of Florie Annie Steele's "The Barber's Wife," from *Tales of the Punjab* (1917).

THE GIANT CATERPILLAR

Long, long ago there was a caterpillar as fat as an elephant. His mouth was as red as his tail. His body was covered with hair and on his head was a long pointed horn.

One day, Mory, Bamba and Badjina went to the field. On the way, they met the caterpillar, who had spread himself across the road to sleep. The children could not pass.

Bamba, who was very well behaved, greeted him politely, saying, "Good day, Papa."

"M'ba,"* answered the caterpillar and moved aside to let him pass.

Next Mory spoke to him. "Good day, Grandfather. How are you?"

"M'ba," replied the caterpillar and little Mory got his turn to pass.

Then Badjina came forward. He wanted to pass too but he was not a well-behaved boy. He was not polite like his friends. He approached the caterpillar and shouted, "Good day, caterpillar." The caterpillar did not answer. He remained as he was, blocking the road with his long, furry body.

Badjina yelled once more, "Red-mouthed caterpillar, I said good day."

The caterpillar did not answer. He did not budge. Badjina screamed, "Red-tailed caterpillar, I said good day."

At last the caterpillar, looking a little redder than usual, got really angry and HOP!!!! he swallowed Badjina in one gulp.

*Good day, thank you.

Mory and Bamba were very frightened. They hid in the bush and only when the caterpillar was out of sight did they dare to return to the village.

Badjina's father ran to the chieftain. "My son has been eaten by a fat caterpillar!" he moaned.

The chieftain called all the men together. "Bring your guns," he ordered, "all your arrows, your bows. We must find the caterpillar, and when we do, we shall kill him."

The men scurried into the bush. But when they caught sight of the huge caterpillar, when they saw his gigantic red mouth and the long pointed horn on his head, they turned tail, threw away their guns, and rushed headlong to the village without once looking back.

"Why are you running? Where is my son? What's going on?" asked Badjina's mama.

"You couldn't begin to know," answered the chieftain. "That animal is as fat as the 'baobab* de Diamadougou.' His mouth is bigger than a calabash. We are afraid and we are running to save ourselves."

Badjina's mother cried and cried, but the oldest woman of the village comforted her, saying, "Inasmuch as the men can't bring Badjina to you, we women shall go and kill the caterpillar. We shall bring your child home to you."

Quickly the women formed a group. Some carried sticks that pound grain, some brought big wooden cooking spoons, some brought knives that they used to peel yams and others even brought hatchets with which they cut firewood.

As they left the village they made fun of the men. "We women aren't afraid," they said. "We shall bring back the red tail of the caterpillar and the big pointed horn from his head."

After walking for several hours the women found the caterpillar. He was, as always, in the middle of the road. He slept just like a boa constrictor ready to swallow a hind.

Bindou, the most courageous of the women, approached

*The baobab is a large tree native to tropical Africa. It has an exceedingly thick trunk and bears a gourdlike fruit.

62

"We women shall go and kill the
caterpillar!" they cried.

the caterpillar on tiptoe. She took one step, two steps, three steps until she was almost on top of the animal. Then she raised her grain-pounding stick very high, then higher, and even higher and...pow!...with one tremendous whack she finished him off. "Everybody, everybody come. Come quickly!" she shouted.

The women came running...thump!...thump!...thump!

The caterpillar is dead!" they shrilled with excitement. "Let us open the belly quickly."

And do you know what they found? Little Badjina, alive and unharmed.

The women cut strong vines from the bushes and tied the caterpillar up. Then they dragged the animal back to the village.

"Look, look," they called, "we have found Badjina and he is alive. We women have killed the caterpillar."

"Cut him up in bits," cried all the others.

Alas, with each cut of the knife, ten, a hundred, a thousand little caterpillars issued forth from the body of the fat animal. They crawled on the ground in the streets in the village square and even in the houses.

And that is why, even today, we find caterpillars everywhere on the earth.

This story from the Republic of the Ivory Coast was told by William Kaufman in the *Unicef Book of Children's Legends* (1970).

THE LAIRD'S LASS AND
THE GOBHA'S SON

An old laird had a young daughter once, and she was the pawkiest lass in all the world. Her father petted her and her mother cosseted her till the wonder of it was that she wasn't so spoiled that she couldn't be borne. What saved her from it was that she was so sunny and sweet by nature, and she had a merry way about her that won all hearts. Nonetheless, when she set her heart on something she'd not give up till she got what it was she wanted.

Nobody minded so much while she was a wee thing, but when she was getting to be a young lady, that's when the trouble began.

She turned out better than anyone would have expected, considering all. You wouldn't have found a bonnier lass if you searched far and wide. But she was as stubborn as ever about having her own way.

Well, now that she was old enough the laird decided it was time to be finding a proper husband for her to wed, so he and her mother began to look about for a suitable lad.

It didn't take long for the lass to find out what they had in mind. She began to do a bit of looking around on her own. She hadn't the shade of a bit of luck at first. All the men who came to the castle were too fat or too thin or too short or too tall or else they were wed already. But she kept on looking just the same.

It was a good thing for her that she did, because one day, as she stood at the window of her bedroom, she saw the lad she could fancy in the courtyard below.

She called to her maid, "Come quick to the window! Who is the lad down below?"

The maid came and looked. "Och, 'tis only the son of the gobha* that keeps the shop in the village. No doubt the laird sent for him about shoeing the new mare," she said. And she went back to her work.

"How does it come that I ne'er saw him before?" asked the lass.

"The gobha's shop is not a place a young lady would be going to at all. Come away from the window now! Your mother would be in a fine fret could she see you acting so bold."

And no doubt she was right, for the lass was hanging over the windowsill.

The lass came away as she was told, but she had made up her mind to go down to the village and get another look at the gobha's son.

She liked the jaunty swing to his kilt, and she liked the way his yellow hair swept back from his brow, and she had a good idea there'd be a lot of other things about him she'd be liking, could she be where she could get a better look at him.

She knew she wouldn't be let go if she asked, so she just went without asking. And to make sure nobody'd know her, she borrowed the dairymaid's Sunday frock and bonnet. She didn't ask for the loan of them either, but just took them away when nobody was around to see.

The gobha's shop was a dark old place, but it wasn't so dark that she couldn't see the gobha's son shoeing the laird's new mare.

His coat was off and his arms were bare and he had a great smudge of soot on his cheek, but she liked what she saw of him even better than before.

He was holding the mare's leg between his knees and fix-

*A gobha is a blacksmith.

66

ing the new shoe on its hoof, so she waited till he finished. Then she stepped inside.

"Good day," said she.

"Good day," said he, looking up in surprise. And he gave her a wide smile that fair turned her heart upside down.

So she gave him one as good in return. "I'm from the castle," said she. "I just stopped in as I passed by to see how you were coming on with the mare."

"I've two shoes on and two to go," said he. "Bide here a bit and I'll ride you up on her back when I'm done."

"Och, nay!" said the laird's daughter. "I just stopped by. They'll be in a taking if I'm late coming home."

Though he begged her to stay, she would not. So off she went.

He was not well pleased to see her go for he'd taken a terrible fancy to her and wanted to know her better. It was only after she was gone that he remembered he'd never asked her name.

When he took the mare back, he tried to find out which of the maids from the castle had been in the village that day. But there were maids galore in the castle and half a dozen or more had been in the village on one errand or another, so he got no satisfaction. He had to go home and hope he'd be seeing her soon again. Whoever she was and wherever she was, she'd taken his heart along with her.

The laird's daughter had come home and put the dairymaid's frock and bonnet back where she got them. After she made herself tidy, she went to find her father. She found him with her mother in the second-best parlor and she stood before them and said, "You can just stop looking for a husband for me to wed because I've found the one I want myself."

The laird laughed, for he thought it a joke she was making, but he soon found out it was not.

"I'm going to marry the gobha's son!" said she.

The laird flew into a terrible rage. But no matter what he said, it was all of no use. The lass had made up her mind, and he couldn't change it for her. And it was no use bothering the gobha's son about it, because he didn't even know who she was. He'd just tell the laird he'd never laid eyes on his daughter.

Well, the laird could only sputter and swear, and his lady could only sit and cry, and the lass was sent to bed without her supper. But the cook smuggled it up to her on a tray, so that did her no harm at all.

The next morning the laird told her that she and her mother were going to Edinbro' in a week's time. And there she'd stay until she was safely wed to her second cousin twice-removed that he'd finally picked to be her husband. The cousin had asked for her hand before, but the laird had been putting him off in case someone better came along. But the way things were, the laird had decided he'd better take the cousin after all, and get his daughter wedded to a husband her mother and he had picked for her themselves.

"I'll go if I must," said the lass. "But you can tell my cousin that I'll not be marrying him. I've made up my mind to wed the gobha's son!"

The gobha's son was having his own troubles.

When the laird and his family came out of the church on the Sabbath morn, they passed by the gobha and his son at the gate. When they'd gone by, the gobha's son pulled at his father's arm.

"Who is the lass with the laird and his lady?" he asked his father.

His father turned and looked. "Och, you ninny!" said he in disgust. "Can you not see 'tis no lass at all? 'Tis a young lady, so it is! That's the laird's own daughter."

The gobha's son had been building cloud-castles about the lass he'd thought was one of the castle maids, and now they all tumbled down. His heart was broken because he was so unlucky as to fall in love with the daughter of the laird.

Well, the days went by till it came to the one before the lass and her mother were to go to Edinbro'. The lass rose from her bed at break of dawn and dressed herself and tiptoed down the stairs. Since this was going to be her last day at home, she wanted to have a little time to be alone for it seemed that either the laird or her mother or else her maid was at her elbow ever since she'd told them she meant to wed the gobha's son.

The cook was in the kitchen as she passed through to the back of the castle. The cook was picking something up from the floor.

"What have you there?" asked the lass.

"'Tis a bairn's wee shoe," said the cook. "One of the laird's dogs fetched it in and dropped it on the floor just now as he went through. It must belong to one of the gardener's weans. 'Tis a bonny wee shoe and much too good for the likes of them," she added with a sniff.

"Give it to me," said the lass. "I'll find the bairn that owns it." She took the shoe and dropped it in her pocket.

Around the stables she went, and through the kitchen garden to the lane that led to the gardener's house. Halfway there she came upon a wee old man sitting on the bank at the side of the lane with his head in his hands. He was crying as if his heart would break. He was the smallest manikin ever she'd seen. He was no bigger than a bairn and indeed he looked so like a bairn, sitting there and weeping so sorely, that she sat down beside him and put her arms about him to comfort him. "Do not greet so sore," said she. "Tell me your trouble and if I can I'll mend it."

"'Tis my shoe!" wept the wee man. "I took it off to take out a stone that got in it, and a great rough dog snatched it from my hand and ran off with it. I cannot walk o'er the briers and brambles and the cruel sharp stones without my shoes and I'll ne'er get home today."

"Well now!" said the lass, with a laugh. "It seems I can mend your troubles easier than my own. Is this what you're weeping for?" And she put her hand in her pocket and took out the shoe she had taken from the cook.

"Och, aye!" cried the wee man. "'Tis my bonny wee shoe!" He caught it from her hand and put it on and, springing into the road, he danced for joy. But in a minute he was back, sitting on the bank beside her.

"Turnabout is only fair," said he. "What are your troubles? Happen I can mend them as you did mine."

"Mine are past mending," said the lass. "For they're taking me to Edinbro' in the morn, to wed my second cousin twice-removed. But I'll not do it. If I can't marry the gobha's son, I'll marry no man at all. I'll lay down and die before I wed another!"

"Och, aye!" said the wee man thoughtfully. "So you want to marry the gobha's son. Does the gobha's son want to wed you?"

"He would if he knew me better," the lass said.

"I could help you," the manikin told her, "but you might have to put up with a bit of inconvenience. You mightn't like it."

"Then I'll thole* it," the lass said. "I'd not be minding anything if it came right for me in the end."

"Remember that," said the wee man laughing, "when the right time comes."

Then he gave her two small things that looked like rowan berries, and told her to swallow them before she slept that night.

"You can leave the rest to me," said he with a grin. "You'll not be going to Edinbro' in the morn!"

When the night came, what with packing and getting ready for the next day's journey, all in the castle went to bed early, being tired out. The laird locked the door of his daughter's room lest the lass take it into her head to run away during the night.

Early the next morn, the maid came up with the lass's breakfast tray. Since the door was locked, she had to put the tray down and go fetch the key from the laird's room.

"I'll come with you," the lass's mother said to the maid. So she got the key from under the laird's pillow and unlocked the lass's door. When she opened the door and went in, she screamed and fainted away. The maid behind her looked to see why, and

*To thole is to endure.

the tray dropped out of her hands. The laird heard the racket and came running. He rushed into the room, and there was his wife on the floor, and the maid, with the tray and the dishes and all at her feet, wringing her hands. He looked at the bed. His daughter wasn't there!

"She's flummoxed us!" said the laird. "Where can she have gone to!"

He and the maid got the laird's wife into a chair and brought her to. The first thing she said was, "Have you looked at the bed?"

"I have!" said the laird grimly. "The pawky lass! She's got away. The bed's empty."

"My love," said his wife weakly. "'Tis not empty."

The laird went over to the bed and his lady came with him. The bed was not empty, though his daughter was not in it.

In her place, with its head on the pillow and its forelegs on the silken coverlet, lay a wee white dog!

"What is that dog doing in my daughter's bed?" shouted the laird. "Put the beastie out in the hall at once!" And he made to do it himself. But his wife caught his arm.

"I do not think it is a dog," she said. "I very much fear the wee dog is our daughter."

"Havers!" the laird said angrily. "Have you all gone daft?"

But they pointed out to him that the doggie was wearing the blue silk nightgown that her mother's own hands had put on her daughter last night. And hadn't the maid braided her young lady's hair and tied it with a blue satin ribbon? Well then, to look at the wee dog's forelock all braided and tied the same, 'twas plain to see that someone had put a spell on the lass and turned her into a dog.

"Nonsense!" said the laird in a rage. "Are you telling me I do not know my daughter from a dog?" And he strode over to the bed. But when he leaned over to pluck the animal from the covers, it looked up at him. The laird looked back in horror, for he saw that the eyes were his daughter's own, and the grin on its face was uncommonly like his lass's own wide naughty

71

smile. And around its neck was the golden chain with the locket he'd given her long ago that she'd worn since he put it there.

But the laird would not admit it. 'Twas all a trick! So he made them search the room from corner to corner and in every cupboard and press. He looked up the chimney himself and got himself covered with smuts, but all he saw was the blue sky above the chimney pot. She was not in the room. She couldn't have got out the windows. She couldn't have gone through the door, for he'd had the key to it. So it all came to this—the wee dog in the bed was his daughter.

He went over to have another look and as he bent down, the little dog chuckled with his daughter's own pleased chuckle and patted him on the cheek just as his daughter used to do. That settled it.

"Och, you wee rascal!" said the laird, never being able to find it in his heart to be angry with his daughter. "Now what are we to do?" There was one thing that was certain and sure. They'd not be going to Edinbro' that day. So a messenger was sent to the second cousin twice-removed, to tell him that he needn't be expecting them. The servants were told the lass was down in bed with some sort of an illness, and nobody but her maid was to be let come into the room lest they catch it. That was enough to keep them all away.

The laird had his own physician come from Edinbro' though his wife told him 'twould do no good at all. He made the man promise not to tell what he saw, then took him into his daughter's room. The doctor look and shook his head. Then he looked at the dog again and rubbed his eyes. "'Tis strange!" he muttered. "I do not see a young lady. I see naught but a wee white dog."

"You see a dog because there is a dog!" shouted the laird.

"'Tis an optical delusion! Begging your lairdship's pardon, your lairdship's daughter is not a dog," insisted the doctor.

"'Tis my daughter," the laird roared. "And she is a dog. So be off with you!"

Well, the maid and his wife were right. The doctor was no use at all. He went back to Edinbro' and wrote a learned paper called "Remarkable Manifestation of Hallucination in A____-shire," which was read by learned societies all over the world, but didn't help the laird at all.

Then the maid suggested they send for an old wife she'd heard of. The old woman came with herbs and powders, but all she could do was tell them the lass had been bewitched. How to take the spell off, she didn't know at all.

The laird was fair distracted, her ladyship took to her bed, and the maid went about in tears from morn till night. All the servants in the castle said it must be a mortal illness the young lady had on her, and they tippy-toed and grieved as they went about their work.

The maids carried the news to the village, and the gobha's son soon heard all about it. If he thought his heart was broken before, it was twice as bad when he thought the laird's daughter might be about to die. For if she were living, at least he'd have a chance to lay his eyes on her now and again. He felt he couldn't be expected to bear it.

He was hammering away at a bit of metal his father had told him to make a brace of, not even noticing the iron had gone cold, when a shadow fell across the door. He looked up and there was the strangest sight he'd ever seen in his life. A wee bit of a man was there all dressed in green from his neck to his heels, and his shoes and his cap were red. He was mounted on a horse so small it could have stood under the belly of any horse the gobha's son had ever seen before, but it was the right size for the wee man in green.

The gobha's son stared, while the wee man got down from his horse and led it into the shop.

"Gobha," said the wee man. "Can you shoe my horse?"

"I'm not the gobha," said the lad. "I'm the gobha's son, and I can shoe your horse. 'Twill take me a while, for I've ne'er shod a beast so small before and I've no notion of the size the shoes must be."

"'Tis no matter," said the wee man. "I've time galore. I'll sit and gab a bit with you till the task is done."

So he made himself comfortable in a corner beyond the forge, and crossing his knees with an easy air, he started to talk to the gobha's son.

It was plain to see that the lad was in no mood for talking. The wee man said the weather had been fine for the time of the year. The lad said only, "Aye. Is it?"

Then the man in green said the fishing was good, he'd heard. To that the lad said happen it was. He wouldn't be knowing.

Then the manikin tried him on the fair in the market town over the hill, but the gobha's son only sighed and said nothing at all.

It was taking a long time, as he said it would, for the horse's hooves were small beyond believing. Shoe after shoe had to be thrown back because they were all too big. But at last he got a set that would fit, and putting the horse where the light fell best, he started to put the horseshoes on its feet.

I'll get you talking yet, my lad, the wee man said to himself.

So, when the gobha's son started to put the shoe on the wee nag's foot, the manikin said, "Have you e'er seen the bonny daughter of the laird up at the castle?"

The gobha's son jumped as if he'd been stuck with a pin. But all he said was, "Aye."

The wee man waited until the lad finished putting the first shoe on. When he picked up the second leg and started to fix the second shoe to the hoof, the wee man asked, "Has anyone told you that she's mortal ill?"

The gobha's son gave a great big sigh, but all he said was, "Aye."

He finished with that shoe and went around to the other side of the wee horse. When he looked to be well started on the third shoe, the man in green asked, "Have you no been up to the castle to ask about the laird's bonny daughter?"

74

The gobha's son shot him a glowering look. "Nay," said he.

That took care of the chatting between the two until the horse was nearly shod. As he was about to fix the last nail in the last of the shoes, the man in green said, "Would you be knowing what ails the bonny young lady?"

The gobha's son waited until he had finished his work and the horse stood with shoes on all four feet. Then he turned to the wee man and he said, "Nay!" He threw the hammer he'd been using aside and told the wee man, "There's your horse all shod and well shod. Now will you take it and yourself away and leave me in peace?"

The wee man stayed where he was. "Not yet!" said he with a grin. "Why do you not go up to the castle and cure the laird's bonny daughter yourself?"

"Cure her!" shouted the gobha's son. "I'd lay down my life to cure her, the bonny young thing." And he asked the wee man furiously, "How could the likes of me do any good when they've had the old wife with her herbs and simples, and the best physician come all the way from Edinbro', and neither of them could set her on her feet again?"

"Whisht, lad!" the manikin scolded. "Would you have all the village running to see what the matter can be? To be sure, they couldn't help her. But I know a way you could cure her. If you'd want to."

As soon as the gobha's son heard that, he was at the wee man to tell him, so that he could run to the castle at once and cure the laird's daughter of her illness.

"Answer me this first," the green manikin said. "Would you like to wed the bonny young lady?"

"Are you daft?" groaned the lad. "Who ever heard of a gobha's son wedding the daughter of a laird?"

"'Tis not what I asked you," said the wee man. "Look, lad! Would you like to wed her?"

"Before I'd wed with anyone else, I'd just lay down and die!" cried the gobha's son.

"'Tis just what the laird's daughter said about yourself,"

75

said the wee man with a satisfied grin. "So, since you are both of the same mind, I'll help you!" Then the wee green man told the gobha's son what he and the lass had been up to.

"Och, nay!" said the lad, "'tis beyond believing."

"It all started because she made up her mind to wed the gobha's son," said the manikin. "So let's you and me be finishing it!"

The wee man gave him two wee things, like rowan berries, as like the ones he'd given the lass as they could be.

"Here's the cure for what ails her," he told the gobha's son.

The lad was all for rushing off to the castle at once, but the wee man held him back.

"Will you be going up to the castle the way you are with your leather apron and soot from the forge all over you?" he scolded. "Och, they'd run you off the place e'er you got the first word in. Tidy yourself first, lad!"

So the lad went and cleaned himself up and got into his Sunday clothes, and a fine figure he was, to be sure. 'Twas no wonder the laird's daughter had set her heart upon him!

"Go with my blessing," said the wee man. "But remember! Don't cure the lass till the laird has given his promise that you can wed her."

"That I'll not!" said the gobha's son. He squared his shoulders, and off he marched to the castle.

The wee man got on his wee horse's back and where he rode to, nobody knows.

Things at the castle were in a terrible state. The laird was at his wit's end. The laird's wife and the castle servants had wept till the walls of the castle were damp with the moisture from their tears. The laird's daughter was getting tired of being a dog, and beginning to fear that she'd ne'er be anything else for the rest of her life. She had snapped at the laird's hand that morning because she was cross with him for not letting her wed the gobha's son in the first place. 'Twas a weary day for the old laird.

The gobha's son walked up to the front door and asked to see the laird. He had such a masterful way with him the ser-

76

vants let him in at once. In no time at all there he was, face to face with the laird.

The laird had left his manners off for the time. "Well who are you and what do you want?" he asked with a frown.

"I'm the gobha's son," said the lad. When the laird heard who it was, he jumped from his chair and started for the lad, ready to throw him out with his own two hands. Because it was the gobha's son who was at the bottom of all the trouble.

The gobha's son sidestepped the laird and said quickly, "And I've come to cure your daughter."

Och, now! That made a difference. Where the laird had been all wrath and scowls, he was now all smiles. He caught the lad by the arm and said, "A hundred thousand welcomes! Come, let's be going to her then."

"Nay," said the lad. "I must know first what I'll get for it."

"Do not let that fash you," the laird said eagerly. "Och, I'll give you a whole big bag of gold. Or two if you like. Come. Let's be at it!"

"'Tis not gold I want," said the lad.

"What is it, then?" the laird asked impatiently.

"Your leave to marry your daughter," said the lad as bold as brass.

"Nay!" thundered the laird. "That you shan't have."

"Then I'll bid you good day," said the gobha's son, and started for the door.

But he never got there. The laird was beside him before he laid his hand on the door knob.

What could the poor old laird do? He had to give in and he knew it. So he did.

"You can have her," said the laird to the gobha's son.

The wee dog jumped from the bed and ran up to the gobha's son the minute he and the laird came into the room. The lad took the berries from his pocket and popped them into her mouth and she swallowed them down. Before you could say, "two two's," there stood the laird's daughter in the wee dog's place!

She took the lad's hand in her own and she turned to the

laird and said, "I'm going to wed the gobha's son."

"Wed him then!" said the laird, not too unhappy about it since he'd got his lass back again. "But you'd better go tell your mother and the maids, so they can stop crying if you want the castle dried out by the time of your wedding."

So the pawky lass got her way in the end and married the gobha's son. The laird was not ill pleased for he found his son-in-law as likeable a body as any he'd ever found. So he made him steward of his estates and a good one the lad was, too. So it all ended well and that's all there is to tell about the laird's daughter and the gobha's son.

"Wee Man" is one of the names given to the smaller Celtic fairies—the pixies, leprechauns, and hobgoblins. They are inclined to be friendly to humans and to repay favors. This is reprinted from *Thistle and Thyme* (1962) by Sorche Nic Leodhas.

THE HUNTED HARE

Once upon a time there was an old woman who lived by herself on the edge of the great wild moor. Many tales the folk thereabouts told of fiends, and spirits, and all manner of fearful things that roamed the moor at night. You may be sure they took care never to be abroad on that bleak stretch of lonely land once darkness had fallen.

Now it happened the old woman had to cross the moor once a week to reach the market town to sell her butter and eggs. She usually rose early, just before dawn, to set out. One night, knowing the next day to be market day, she went to bed quite early. When she awoke, she began to get ready for her journey. It was still dark of course, and, having no clock, she did not know it was still before midnight. She dressed, ate, saddled her horse, and attached to it the large wicker panniers containing the butter and eggs. Wrapping a worn old cloak about her, she and the horse sleepily set off across the moor.

She had not gone very far before she heard the sounds of a pack of hounds baying under the stars and saw, racing toward her, a white hare. When it reached her, the hare leaped up on a large rock close by the path as if to say, "Come, catch me."

The old woman chuckled. She liked the idea of outwitting the hounds, so she reached out her hand, picked up the crouching hare, and popped it into one of her wicker panniers. She dropped the lid and rode on.

The baying of the hounds came nearer, and suddenly she saw a headless horse galloping toward her, surrounded by a pack of monstrous hounds. On the horse sat a dark figure with horns sprouting out of his head. The eyes of the hounds shone fiery red, while their tails glowed with a blue flame.

It was a terrifying sight to behold. Her horse stood trembling and shaking, but the woman sat up boldly to confront the horned demon. She had the hare in her basket and didn't intend to give it up. But it seemed that these monstrous creatures were not very clever or knowing, for the rider asked the old woman, very civilly, had she seen a white hare run past and did she know in which direction it had gone.

"No indeed," she said firmly. "I saw no hare run past me." Which of course was true.

The rider spurred his headless horse, called his hounds to follow, and galloped across the moors. When they were out of sight, the woman patted and calmed her shivering horse.

Suddenly, to her surprise, the lid of the pannier moved and then opened. It was no frightened hare who came forth, but a woman all in white.

The ghostly lady spoke in a clear voice. "Dame," she said, "I admire your courage. You have saved me from a terrible enchantment and now the spell is broken. I am no human woman —it was my fate to be condemned for centuries to the form of a hare and to be pursued on the moor at night by evil demons, until I could get behind their tails while they passed on in search of me. Through your courage the enchantment is broken, and I can now return to my own kind. We will never forget you. I promise that all your hens shall lay two eggs instead of one, your cows shall give plenty of milk year round, your garden crops shall thrive and yield a fine harvest. But beware the devil fiend and his evil spirits, for he will try to do you harm once he realizes you were clever enough to outwit him. May good fortune attend you."

The mysterious lady vanished and was never seen again, but all she promised came true. The woman had the best possible luck at market that morning and continued to have good fortune with all her crops and livestock. The devil never did

"No, indeed," the old woman said firmly.
"I saw no hare run past me."

succeed in getting revenge—though he had many a try—and the kindly protection of the ghostly lady stayed with the woman the rest of her life.

Originally "White Ladies" were early pagan deities who gave fertility to land and livestock; now they are thought of as Celtic ghosts or fairies. Headless horses and mounstrous, baying hounds appear in folk tales from the southwest of England and were used by Conan Doyle in his *Hound of the Baskervilles.* The editor's source for this retelling was Hartland's *English Fairy and Folk Tales* (1890).

THE YOUNG HEAD OF
THE FAMILY

Long ago in China there lived an old farmer with three sons. Two of the sons who had recently married brought their wives home, and all lived together as a family. Since there was no mother in the household, every time the young wives wanted to visit their parents and relatives in another village they had to ask their husbands' father if they might go, for this was the custom at that time.

They asked to visit their relatives so often that the old farmer became very annoyed.

"You are always asking me to let you go off to visit your relatives," he said. "When I refuse you think me very hardhearted. Very well, you may go, but only on the condition that you each bring me back what I ask."

"Yes, of course," they said quickly.

"One of you must bring me fire wrapped in paper, and the other must bring me wind in paper. If you cannot do that, do not come back!"

The young wives agreed without thinking and happily set out to walk the long distance to their own village.

On the way one of the wives' sandal straps broke, and they sat down by the roadside to fix it. Only then did they realize that it would be impossible to bring back wind in paper or fire wrapped in paper. They sat by the roadside in despair, for they did not want to leave their husbands.

Along came a girl riding a water buffalo. Seeing their unhappy faces, she asked if she could help them.

"No one can help us!" they cried. "What our husbands'

father asks is impossible!"

But the girl insisted that she might be able to help, and at last they told her their story.

"Come home with me, and I will show you how to bring him what he asks," said the girl.

Off they went with her to her home, where she showed them a paper lantern with a candle inside. "There, you see, is fire in paper, and here," she said picking up a paper fan and waving it, "is wind in paper."

The young women thanked her and went happily on their way. After a cheerful visit with relatives and friends in their villages, they took a paper lantern and a fan and returned to their husbands.

"I told you not to return unless you brought the two things I asked for," said the old farmer sharply.

"But we have them," they answered. And they gave him the paper lantern and the fan.

The old man was astonished. "Tell me how you solved this riddle!" he demanded.

Then they told him of meeting the young girl on the water buffalo, and the advice she had given them.

"That is a very clever young woman," the old farmer thought. "She would make a good wife for my youngest son."

So he at once set about finding out if the young girl was already betrothed. Upon learning that she was not, he sent a matchmaker to her family to arrange the marriage.

All the arrangements took place as planned, and after the marriage celebration was over, the old farmer said to his family, "Since the wife of my youngest son is so wise, she will now be the head of the family. You must ask her advice and direction in all things."

The new, young head of the household told the men of the family they must neither go to the fields, nor return home, empty-handed. Each day they were to bring fertilizer of some kind from the farm buildings to the fields, and each day gather sticks of firewood on their return.

In this way their crops thrived, and the family always had a supply of firewood. When there were only a few sticks to gather, they were told to bring back stones. Soon, near the house, there was a pile of stones that could be used for building.

One day a gem dealer came riding by and stopped to examine the pile of stones. Among them he saw a stone that contained a block of precious jade.

He at once went to the house and asked to talk to the head of the family. He was, of course, surprised to see so young a woman, but so skillfully did she manage the bargaining that he finally agreed to pay a very high price for the pile of stones. He said nothing about the jade among the stones, but he promised to return in three days time with the money.

That night the young wife thought about the matter and decided the heap of stones must contain some kind of valuable gem.

She went to her father-in-law and told him to invite the dealer to dinner. Then she advised the men of the family to talk about precious stones and how they could be recognized when found on the ground.

While the men feasted and talked, the young head of the family listened behind a curtain. When she had the information she needed, she went outside to the pile of stones and found the one that was valuable. Then she brought it into the house and put it away.

The next day the dealer returned and discovered the valuable jade was no longer there. He realized his trick had been discovered, and he sought out the young head of the family. Again she bargained firmly with the dealer. She would not agree to sell the jade unless he also bought the pile of building stones, and after long discussion, she secured a proper payment for both.

The old farmer and his family were very proud of her business ability. They were now prosperous and decided to build a much larger, more comfortable new home. Inscribed on the gateway to the new house were the words, "No Sorrow."

Not long afterward a mandarin* came by and, seeing the

*A mandarin is a Chinese government official.

unusual words over the entrance, ordered his servants to set down his sedan chair.

"That is a very arrogant motto," said he with displeasure. "No family is without sorrow! You mock the gods, and I shall fine you for this impudence."

"This family has been fortunate and happy," the young head of the household answered politely. "The words 'no sorrow' mean let all who enter here leave sorrow at the gate."

The mandarin was not appeased. "I order you to weave me a piece of cloth as long as this road!"

"Very well," she answered. "As soon as Your Excellency has found the two ends of the road and told me the exact number of feet in its length, I will at once begin weaving."

The mandarin knew he had been at fault in hastily imposing such a fine, but he was irritated at the young woman's clever answer. He added angrily, "And I also fine you as much oil as there is water in the sea."

"Certainly," she answered. "As soon as you have measured the sea and sent me the correct number of gallons, I will begin to press out the oil from my beans."

"Since you are so clever and witty, perhaps you can read my mind!" he snapped. "If you can, I withdraw the fines. I hold this pet bird in my hand. Now tell me whether I mean to squeeze it to death or to let it fly in the air."

"Well," said the young woman. "I am an obscure commoner, and you are a famous official. If you are no more knowing than I, you have no right to fine me at all. Now, I stand with one foot on the one side of my threshold and the other foot on the other side. Tell me whether I mean to go in or come out. If you cannot guess my mind, you should not require me to guess yours."

Of course, the mandarin could not guess her intention, and was forced to admit to himself the wisdom of her words. He haughtily took his departure, and the family lived happily ever after under its chosen head.

Kate Douglas Wiggin retold this Chinese tale in 1908. It is a Chinese version of the clever woman who solves riddles, retold once more by the editor.

THE LEGEND OF KNOCKMANY

Long ago, in Ireland, there lived a giant named Cucullin. No other giant of the time was his equal in size or strength, not even the famed Fin M'Coul. 'Twas said no other giant had a chance with Cucullin in a fight. So powerfully strong was he that, when angry, he could stamp his foot and shake the whole countryside around him. With one blow of his fist he had flattened a thunderbolt in the shape of a pancake and kept it in his pocket to frighten his enemies. Truth to tell, he liked being the most feared giant in Ireland. He had beaten up every other giant in the land—every one, that is, save Fin M'Coul. As for Fin, Cucullin swore he would never rest until he had caught up with him and knocked him senseless.

Now Fin was not nearly as big a giant as Cucullin, but he was brash and cocky, and he had given out that he'd wipe the ground with Cucullin if ever he had the luck to meet up with him. But Fin, who was no fool, took care to stay well clear of Cucullin.

So matters stood one fine spring day when Fin and his men were up north working on the Giant's Causeway to Scotland. When news came to Fin that Cucullin was headed that way to have a trial of strength with him, Fin was seized with a sudden desire to visit his wife Oonagh. So he pulled up a fir tree, lopped off the branches to make a walking stick of it, and set off at once for his home at Knockmany.

In truth, people wondered why he had built his house at the top of Knockmany, where the winds blew fiercely from every direction and there was not a drop of water. Oonagh had to go down to a spring at the foot of the steep hill and then carry her full pails up to the top again.

"There's a fine prospect in every direction," was Fin's answer. "And as for the water, I plan to sink a well up on top one of these days when I get around to it." He'd been saying this for many years, but of course the real reason for living on top of Knockmany was so that he could keep a sharp lookout for Cucullin or any other enemy headed his way.

"God save all here!" said Fin as he put his face in the door.

"Welcome home, you darlin'," cried Oonagh. Fin then gave her such a warm smack on the lips that the waters in the lake across the valley curled and bounced.

Fin spent two or three happy days with Oonagh feeling very comfortable, except for the dread he had of Cucullin. But Oonagh soon sensed that something was troubling him.

"What is it with you now?" she asked.

"It's that beast Cucullin," brooded Fin, and he popped his thumb into his mouth. Now Fin's thumb had a magical property. When he put it into his mouth and touched a special tooth, it could tell him what was going to happen.

"He's coming this way," said Fin looking as miserable as a wet sock, "and what to do I don't know. If I run away I am disgraced and a laughing stock to all the other giants. Sooner or later I must meet him, my thumb tells me so. But how to fight with a giant that makes a pancake out of a thunderbolt and shakes the whole country with a stamp of his foot? He'll make mincemeat out of me, he will!"

"When will he be here?" asked Oonagh.

"Tomorrow, about two o'clock," groaned Fin.

"Don't fret yourself," she answered. "Depend on me and we'll settle this once and for all. I'll bring you out of this scrape better than you could yourself, by your rule of thumb."

Fin became very melancholy. Strong and brave though he was, what chance would he have against that ugly customer Cucullin? "What can you do for me, Oonagh, with all your invention? Sure I'll be skinned like a rabbit before your eyes. I'll be disgraced in the sight of my tribe, and me the best man among them!"

"Be easy now, Fin," she said. "Thunderbolt pancakes he fancies, does he? You just leave him to me and do as I bid."

This relieved Fin very much, for he had great confidence in his wife who had gotten him out of many a pickle before this. Oonagh went to the skeins of wool hanging outside to dry and drew nine long strands of different colors. She then plaited the wool into three plaits with three colors in each, putting one around her right arm, one around her right ankle, and the third around her chest over her heart. Now she knew she would not fail in anything she undertook.

Next she went round to her neighbors and borrowed twenty-one iron griddles, thin round and flat they were. Then she kneaded dough for bread and hid the griddles inside the twenty-one loaves of bread she was shaping. In addition, she made one round loaf in the regular way, without a griddle hidden inside. While they were baking, she made a large pot of milk cheese. She then made a high smoking fire on the top of the hill, after which she put her fingers in her mouth and gave three whistles. This was the way that the Irish long ago gave a sign to all strangers and travelers to let them know they were welcome.

Having done all this, she sat down that evening, quite contented, and asked Fin to tell her more about Cucullin. One of the things he told her was that Cucullin's middle finger on his right hand was the magical source of his great strength. Should he lose that, he had no more power than a common man, for all his large bulk.

The next day Cucullin was seen striding across the valley, taller than a round tower. Oonagh took out the old cradle and made Fin lie down in it. Then she handed him a white cotton bonnet to tie over his head.

"Curl yourself up and pretend to be your own child," said she covering him with a quilt. "Say nothing now, but be guided by me."

A thunderous knock on the door shook the house. Fin huddled in the cradle and turned pale.

"Come in and welcome," cried Oonagh. Cucullin bent down to enter, for he was a taller giant than old Fin.

"Is this where the famous Fin M'Coul lives?"

"It is," said Oonagh. "Won't you be sitting down?"

"Thank you kindly, I will," said Cucullin. "Is he at home now?"

"Why no," said Oonagh, "he left the house this morning in a perfect fury! Someone told him a big, bragging, gossoon of a giant called Cucullin was looking for him up at the Causeway, and he set off to try to catch him. I hope for the poor giant's sake Fin doesn't catch him, for he'll make a paste of him if he does!"

"Well," said the huge giant, "I am Cucullin and I've been seeking him these twelve months. I'll not stop till I get my hands on him."

Oonagh gave a loud laugh of contempt. "Poor fellow! I'm thinking you've never seen the great Fin M'Coul."

"How could I," said he, "with him dodging about and keeping clear of me?"

"It'll be a bleak day for you if you meet up with Fin," Oonagh replied. "But stay and rest awhile, and we'll hope the wild temper on him will cool down a bit. In the meantime I'll ask a civil favor of you. The wind is blowing in the door from the east. If you'd be kind enough to turn the house around? For that is what Fin does when he's here."

Cucullin stared at her in astonishment. However, he got up and went outside with Oonagh, and after pulling the middle finger of his right hand three times, he lifted the house and turned it around as she wished. Fin in the cradle felt the sweat start out on him, for, of course, this was something he had never done.

Oonagh nodded in satisfaction. "I've always preferred the house this way. Now, since you're out here maybe you'd do one more thing to oblige me?"

"And what's that?" asked Cucullin uneasily.

"After this long spell of dry weather, we're badly off for want of water," replied Oonagh. "Fin says there's a fine spring well under the rocks here. It was his intention to pull them asunder today, but he left in such a rage to find you he didn't have time to do it." And she showed him a crevice in the rocky surface behind the house.

Cucullin looked at it and glowered. It was plain he didn't fancy the job. But he cracked his middle finger nine times and, bending down, he tore a cleft in the rock forty feet deep. Up gushed the spring Oonagh had been needing these many years.

"Thank you kindly," said she, "and now you must come in to share the food I'd prepared for Fin. For even though you're enemies, he'd expect me to make you welcome and share our humble fare."

She brought him in and placed before him a half dozen of the specially prepared round bread loaves, together with a can or two of butter and cheese.

Cucullin put one of the loaves in his mouth and let out a thundering yell.

"What's the matter?" asked Oonagh coolly.

"Matter!" he shouted. "Here are two of my teeth out! What kind of bread is this you've given me?"

"Why," said she, "that's Fin's bread—the only bread he ever eats when he's at home. Nobody else can eat it but himself and his little son in the cradle there. But since you think yourself the equal of Fin, try another loaf. It may not be as hard."

By this time Cucullin was very hungry, so he made a fresh start at the second loaf. This time he gave out a cry louder than the first, for he'd bitten into the loaf harder, not wishing to appear a weakling.

"Thunder and gibbets!" he roared. "Take your bread away or I'll not have a tooth in my head. There's two more teeth out!"

"If you're not able to eat the bread, say so quietly or you'll wake the child in the cradle. There now, he's awake on me!"

Fin gave a skirl that startled the giant, coming from what

he thought was a baby. "Mother," cried Fin, "I'm hungry!" Oonagh brought him the bread loaf that had no griddle in it and put it into his hand. Fin chewed it up and swallowed it.

Cucullin was thunderstruck. He thanked his stars he'd had the good fortune to miss finding Fin at home. "I'd have no chance with him," he thought, "for even his little son can easily chew the bread that breaks my teeth!"

"Is it special teeth they have in Fin's family?" he asked aloud as he got up to leave. He had decided he'd rather not have anything to do with Fin M'Coul.

"Why don't you feel for yourself?" answered Oonagh. I'll get the babe to open his mouth. It's rather far back they are, so put your longest finger in."

Cucullin was surprised to find such a powerful set of grinders in one so young. And even more astounded to find he'd lost the very finger on which his strength depended. With a good hard bite, Fin had taken off his enemy's finger. Cucullin now was powerless.

Fin jumped out of the cradle, and Cucullin, with a shriek of terror, turned to run for it. All the way down the hill he ran, with Fin after him. Fin didn't catch him for Cucullin could still run fast, even if his magical power was gone. So Fin returned up the hill to find Oonagh cutting the iron griddles out of the loaves. He gave her a hug and a smack and they settled down to dinner in peace.

William Carleton published this tale in the early nineteenth century in his collection of stories from Irish peasants. W. B. Yeats reprinted it in his folk tale collection, and J. Jacobs retold it. This version by the editor is based on Jacobs' retelling, although the original tale probably dates from the sixteenth century when comic parodies of the ancient heroic legends developed.

KUPTI AND IMANI

Once there was a king who had two daughters and their names were Kupti and Imani. He loved them both very much and spent hours in talking to them.

One day he said to Kupti, the elder, "Are you satisfied to leave your life and fortune in my hands?"

"Verily, yes," answered the princess, surprised at the question. "In whose hands should I leave them, if not in yours?"

But when he asked his daughter Imani the same question, she replied, "No, indeed! If I had the chance I would make my own fortune."

At this answer the king was very displeased, and said, "You are too young to know the meaning of your words. But, be it so, my daughter, I will give you the chance of gratifying your wish."

Then he sent for an old lame fakir* who lived in a tumble-down hut on the outskirts of the city, and when he had presented himself, the king said, "No doubt, as you are very old and nearly crippled, you would be glad to have some young person live with you and serve you; so I will send you my younger daughter. She wants to earn her living and she can do so with you."

Of course the old fakir had not a word to say; or if he had, he was really too astonished and troubled to say it. But the young princess went off with him smiling, and tripped along quite gaily, while he hobbled home with her in perplexed silence.

*A fakir is a beggar.

93

Directly they reached the hut the old man began to think what he could arrange for the princess's comfort. But after all he was a beggar, and his house was bare except for one bedstead, two old cooking pots and an earthen jar for water, and one cannot get much comfort out of such things.

However, the princess soon ended his perplexity by asking, "Have you any money?"

"I have a penny somewhere," replied the fakir.

"Very well," rejoined the princess, "give me the penny and go out and borrow me a spinning wheel and a loom."

After much seeking the fakir found the penny and started on his errand, while the princess went shopping. First she bought a farthing's worth of oil, and then she bought three farthings' worth of flax. When she returned with her purchases, she set the old man on the bedstead and rubbed his crippled leg with the oil for an hour.

Then she sat down to the spinning wheel and spun and spun all night long while the old man slept. In the morning, she had spun the finest thread that ever was seen. Next she went to the loom and wove and wove until, by the evening, she had woven a beautiful silver cloth.

"Now," said she to the fakir, "go into the marketplace and sell my cloth while I rest."

"And what am I to ask for it?" said the old man.

"Two gold pieces," replied the princess.

So the fakir hobbled away, and stood in the marketplace to sell the cloth. Presently the elder princess drove by, and when she saw the cloth she stopped and asked the price, for it was better work than she or any of her women could weave.

"Two gold pieces," said the fakir. And the princess gladly paid them, after which the old man hobbled home with the money.

As she had done before, so Imani did again day after day. Always she spent a penny upon oil and flax, always she tended the old man's lame leg, and spun and wove the most beautiful cloths and sold them at high prices. Gradually the city became famous for her beautiful goods, the old fakir's lame leg became straighter and stronger, and the hole under the floor of the hut where they kept their money became fuller and fuller of gold pieces.

At last, one day, the princess said, "I really think we have enough to live on in greater comfort." She sent for builders, and they built a beautiful house for her and the old fakir, and in all the city there was none finer except the king's palace. Presently this reached the ears of the king, and when he inquired whose it was they told him that it belonged to his daughter.

"Well," exclaimed the king, "she said that she would make her own fortune, and somehow or other she seems to have done it!"

A little while after this, business took the king to another country, and before he went he asked his elder daughter what she would like him to bring her back as a gift.

"A necklace of rubies," answered she. And then the king thought he would like to ask Imani too; so he sent a messenger to find out what sort of present she wanted. The man happened to arrive just as she was trying to disentangle a knot in her loom, and bowing low before her, he said, "The king sends me to inquire what you wish him to bring you as a present from the country of Dûr?"

But Imani, who was only considering how she could best untie the knot without breaking the thread, replied, "Patience," meaning that the messenger should wait till she was able to attend to him. But the messenger went off with this as an answer and told the king that the only thing Princess Imani wanted was patience.

"Oh!" said the king. "I don't know whether that's a thing to be bought at Dûr. I never had it myself, but if it is to be found I will buy it for her."

Next day the king departed on his journey, and when his business at Dûr was completed he bought for Kupti a beautiful ruby necklace.

Then he said to a servant, "The Princess Imani wants some

patience. I did not know there was such a thing, but you must go to the market and inquire, and if any is to be sold, get it and bring it to me."

The servant saluted and left the king's presence. He walked about the market for some time crying., "Has anyone patience to sell? Patience to sell?" And some of the people mocked; and some, who had no patience, told him to go away and not be a fool; and some said, "The fellow's mad! As though one could buy or sell patience!"

At length it came to the ears of the King of Dûr that a madman was in the market trying to buy patience. The king laughed and said, "I should like to see that fellow, bring him here!"

And immediately his attendants went to seek the man and brought him to the king, who asked, "What is this you want?"

And the man replied, "Sire, I am bidden to ask for patience."

"Oh," said the king, "you must have a strange master! What does he want with it?"

"My master wants it as a present for his daughter Imani," replied the servant.

"Well," said the king, "I know of some patience which the young lady might have if she cares for it, but it is not to be bought."

Now the king's name was Subbar Khan, and Subbar means patience; but the messenger did not know that, or understand that he was making a joke. However, he declared that Princess Imani was not only young and lovely, but also the cleverest, most industrious, and kindest-hearted of princesses.

And he would have gone on explaining her virtues had not the king laughingly put up his hand and stopped him saying, "Well, well, wait a minute, and I will see what can be done."

With that he rose and went to his own apartments and took out a little casket. Into the casket he put a fan, and shutting it up carefully, he brought it to the messenger and said, "Here is a casket. It has neither lock nor key and yet will open only to the touch of the person who needs its contents—and whoever opens it will obtain patience; but I cannot tell whether it will be the kind of patience that is wanted."

The servant bowed low and took the casket, but when he asked what was to be paid, the king would take nothing. So he went away and gave the casket and an account of his adventures to his master.

As soon as their father returned to his country, Kupti and Imani each received the presents he had brought for them. Imani was very surprised when the casket was brought to her by the hand of a messenger.

"But," she said, "what is this? I never asked for anything! Indeed I had no time, for the messenger ran away before I had unraveled my tangle."

But the servant declared the casket was for her, so she took it with some curiosity and brought it to the old fakir. The old man tried to open it, but in vain—so closely did the lid fit that it seemed to be quite immovable, and yet there was neither lock nor bolt nor spring, nor anything apparently by which the casket was kept shut. When he was tired of trying he handed the casket to the princess, who hardly touched it before it opened quite easily, and there lay within a beautiful fan. With a cry of surprise and pleasure Imani took out the fan and began to fan herself.

Hardly had she finished three strokes of the fan before there suddenly appeared before her King Subbar Khan of Dûr! The princess gasped and rubbed her eyes, and the old fakir sat and gazed in such astonishment that for some minutes he could not speak.

At length he said, "Who may you be, fair sir, if you please?"

"My name," said the king, "is Subbar Khan of Dûr. This lady," bowing to the princess, "has summoned me, and here I am!"

"I?" stammered the princess. "I have summoned you? I never saw or heard of you in my life before, so how could that be?"

Then the king told them how he had heard of a man in his

own city of Dûr trying to buy patience, and how he had given him the fan in the casket.

"Both are magical," he added. "When anyone uses the fan, in three strokes of it I am with her; if she folds it and taps it on the table, in three taps I am at home again. The casket will not open to all, but you see it was this fair lady who asked for patience, and as that is my name, here I am, very much at her service."

Now Princess Imani, being of a high spirit, was anxious to fold up the fan and give the three taps which would send the king home again. But the old fakir was very pleased with his guest, and so in one way and another they spent a pleasant evening together before Subbar Khan took his leave.

After that he was often summoned, and as both the fakir and he were very fond of chess and were good players, they used to sit up half the night playing until at last a little room in the house began to be called the king's room. Whenever he stayed late he slept there and went home again in the morning.

By and by, it came to the ears of Princess Kupti that a rich and handsome young man was visiting at her sister's house, and she was very jealous. So she went one day to pay Imani a visit, pretending to be very affectionate and interested in the house, and in the way in which Imani and the old man lived, and of their mysterious and royal visitor.

As the sisters went from place to place, Kupti was shown Subbar Khan's room. Presently, making some excuse, she slipped in by herself and swiftly spread under the sheet which lay upon the bed a quantity of very finely powdered and splintered glass which was poisoned, and which she had brought with her concealed in her clothes. Shortly afterward she took leave of her sister, declaring she could never forgive herself for not having come near her all this time, and that she would now begin to make amends for her neglect.

That very evening Subbar Khan came and sat up late with the old fakir playing chess as usual. Very tired, he at length bade him and the princess good night, but soon as he lay down

Imani passed through the market crying,
"Medicine for sale!"

on the bed, thousands of tiny, tiny splinters of poisoned glass ran into him. He could not think what was the matter, and turned this way and that until he was pricked all over and felt as though he were burning from head to foot. But he said never a word, only sitting up all night in agony of body and in worse agony of mind to think that he should have been poisoned, as he guessed he was, in Imani's own house.

In the morning, although he was nearly fainting, he still said nothing, and by means of the magic fan was duly transported home again. Then he sent for all the physicians and doctors in his kingdom, but none could make out what his illness was. And so he lingered on for weeks and weeks, trying every remedy that anyone could devise, and passing sleepless nights and days of pain and fever and misery, until at last he was at the point of death.

Meanwhile Princess Imani and the old fakir were much troubled, because, although they waved the magic fan again and again, no Subbar Khan appeared. They feared that he had tired of them, or that some evil fate had overtaken him. At last the princess was in such a miserable state of doubt and uncertainty that she determined to go herself to the kingdom of Dûr and see what was the matter. Disguising herself as a young fakir, she set out upon her journey alone and on foot, as a fakir should travel.

One evening she found herself in a forest and lay down under a great tree to pass the night. But she could not sleep for thinking of Subbar Khan and wondering what had happened to him. Presently she heard two great monkeys talking to one another in the tree above her head.

"Good evening, brother," said one, "whence come you and what is the news?"

"I come from Dûr," said the other, "and the news is that the king is dying."

"Oh," said the first, "I'm sorry to hear that, for he is a master hand at slaying leopards and creatures that ought not to be allowed to live. What is the matter with him?"

"No man knows," replied the second monkey, "but the

100

birds, who see all and carry all messages, say that he is dying of poisoned glass that Kupti, the king's daughter, spread upon his bed."

"Ah," said the first monkey, "that is sad news. But if they only knew it, the berries of the very tree we sit in, steeped in hot water, will cure such a disease as that in three days at most."

"True!" said the other. "It is a pity we cannot tell someone of a medicine so simple, and so save a good man's life. But people are so silly; they go and shut themselves up in stuffy houses in stuffy cities instead of living in nice airy trees, and so they miss knowing all the best things."

Now when Imani heard that Subbar Khan was dying, she began to weep silently. But as she listened she dried her tears and sat up, and as soon as daylight dawned over the forest she began to gather the berries from the tree until she had filled her cloth with a load of them. Then she walked on as fast as she could, and in two days reached the city of Dûr.

The first thing she did was to pass through the market crying, "Medicine for sale! Are any ill that need my medicine?"

And presently one man said to his neighbor, "See, there is a young fakir with medicine for sale. Perhaps he could do something for the king."

"Pooh," replied the other, "where so many graybeards have failed, how should a lad like that be of any use?"

"Still," said the first, "he might try." And he went up and spoke to Imani, and together they set out for the palace and announced that another doctor was come to try and cure the king.

After some delay Imani was admitted to the sick room, and, while she was so well disguised that the king did not recognize her, he was so wasted by illness that she hardly knew him. But she began at once, full of hope, by asking for an apartment all to herself and a pot in which to boil water.

As soon as the water was heated she steeped some of her berries in it and, giving the mixture to the king's attendants, told them to wash his body with it. The first washing did so much good that the king slept quietly all the night. Again the second day she did the same, and this time the king declared he was hungry and called for food. After the third day he was quite well, only very weak from his long illness. On the fourth day he got up and sat upon his throne, and then sent messengers to fetch the physician who had cured him.

When Imani appeared everyone marveled that so young a man should be so clever a doctor, and the king wanted to give him immense presents of money and of all kinds of precious things. At first Imani would take nothing, but at last she said that, if she must be rewarded, she would ask for the king's signet ring and his handkerchief. So, as she would take nothing more, the king gave her his signet ring and his handkerchief, and she departed and traveled back to her own country as fast as she could.

A little while after her return, when she had related to the fakir all her adventures, they sent for Subbar Khan by means of the magic fan. When he appeared they asked him why he had stayed away for so long. Then he told them all about his illness, and how he had been cured. When he had finished, the princess rose up and, opening a cabinet, brought out the ring and handkerchief and said, laughing, "Are these the rewards you gave to your doctor?"

At that the king recognized her and understood in a moment all that had happened, and he jumped up and put the magic fan in his pocket, declaring that no one should send him away to his own country any more unless Imani would come with him and be his wife. And so it was settled, and the old fakir and Imani went to the city of Dûr, where Imani was married to the king and lived happily ever after.

Leonora Alleyne Lang adapted this story from an old tale of the Punjabi area. It appeared in Andrew Lang's *Olive Fairy Book* (1907).

THE LUTE PLAYER

Once upon a time a king and a queen lived quite happily in their small kingdom. The king held tournaments and practiced mock battle with his knights; but after a time he grew bored and restless. He longed to go out into the world to try his skill in battle, and to win fame and glory.

So he called his band of armed knights together and gave orders to start for a distant country where lived a cruel king who raided the countries all around him. The queen, who had always shared the duties of the kingdom, was now given full power to rule in his absence. He commanded his ministers to assist the queen in all things; then, taking tender leave of his wife, the king set out with his small force.

After a time the king reached the lands of the foreign ruler. He rode on until he came to a mountain pass where a large army lay in wait for him. His force was defeated; the king himself was taken prisoner.

He was carried off to the prison where the captives suffered badly. The prisoners were kept chained all night long, and in the morning they were yoked together like oxen to plow the land till it grew dark.

In the meantime the queen governed the land wisely and well. The country remained at peace with its neighbors and her subjects prospered. But when one year became two, and then three, the queen grieved at her husband's long absence. Since no word was received from him, she feared he had been killed.

When at last the poor king was able to send her a message,

her grief turned to joy. The letter told of his capture and gave instructions for his rescue:

"...Sell our castles and estates and borrow money to raise as large a fortune as you can. Either bring or send the gold to ransom me—for that is the only hope of deliverance from this terrible prison...."

The queen pondered the message. She was resolved to obtain his release as quickly as possible, but to raise so large a sum would take many months.

"Then if I bring the ransom gold myself," she thought, "this foreign king might seize the gold and imprison me, too. If I send messengers with the ransom, whom shall I trust? It is a long distance to travel with a cart full of gold! And what then if the ransom offer is refused or seized? This ruthless king may not want to ransom a prisoner—or he may be so wealthy he will laugh at our gold!"

The queen paced her chamber in despair. "If I do as the king requests, he would return home beggared and in debt, the country impoverished." These thoughts filled her mind until she was nearly distracted.

At last an idea came to her. She would journey to the distant land as a vagabond minstrel, a lute player, and she would rescue the king herself. She cut her long brown hair and dressed herself as a minstrel boy. Then she took her lute, and leaving word that she was going on a journey, she left the castle at night. She did not know if her bold plan would succeed; but she knew the ministers would be horrified and detain her if they could.

At first the queen rode alone, but soon she joined a party of pilgrims journeying her way. Later she joined a group of merchants and peddlers. The young minstrel who played the lute so well and sang so gaily was welcome company to the travelers.

In this way she neared her destination in little more than a month. Leaving the party of merchants, she headed for the steep mountain pass and the country where her husband was imprisoned. She had become thin and browned by the sun, and the bright colors of her minstrel cloak were dusty and worn.

When at last she arrived at the palace of the foreign king, she walked all around it and at the back she saw the prison. Then she went into the great court in front of the palace. Taking her lute in her hands, she began to play so artfully that all who heard her felt as though they could never hear enough.

After she had played for some time she began to sing, and her voice was sweeter than the nightingale's:

> I come from my own country far
> Into this foreign land;
> Of all I own, I take alone
> My sweet lute in my hand.
>
> Oh, who will thank me for my song
> Reward my simple lay?*
> Like lovers' sighs it still shall rise
> To greet thee day by day.
>
> My song begs for your pity
> And gifts from out your store;
> And as I play my gentle lay
> I linger near your door.
>
> And if you hear my singing
> Within your palace, sire,
> Oh, give I pray, this happy day,
> To me my heart's desire.

No sooner had the king heard this touching song, sung by such a lovely voice, than he had the singer brought before him.

"Welcome, lute player," said he. "Where do you come from?"

"My country, sire, is far away across many lands. I wander from country to country, and I earn my living with my music."

"Stay here then a few days, and when you wish to leave, I

*A lay is a ballad or song.

105

will give you as reward what you ask for in your song—your heart's desire."

So the lute player stayed on in the palace and played and sang songs both merry and sad. The king, who was charmed and beguiled by the songs and the music, never tired of listening and almost forgot to eat or drink.

After three days the lute player came to take leave of the king.

"Well," said the king, "what do you desire as your reward?"

"Sire, give me one of your prisoners. You have so many in your prison, and I should be glad of a companion on my journeys. When I hear his happy voice as I travel along, I shall think of you and thank you."

"Come along then," said the king, "choose whomever you wish." And he took the lute player through the prison himself.

The queen walked about among the prisoners, and at length she picked out her husband and took him with her on her journey home. Again they traveled the roads with parties of pilgrims and traders, and the king never suspected that the thin, sunbrowned minstrel who entertained the travelers could be his queen.

At last they reached the border of their own country. "Let me go now, kind lad," said her companion. "I am no common prisoner but the king of this country. Let me go free and ask what you will as your reward."

"Do not speak of reward," answered the lute player. "Go in peace."

"Then come with me, friend, and be my guest."

"When the proper time comes I shall be at your palace," said the minstrel, and so they parted.

The queen took a shorter way home, arriving at the castle before the king. She changed her clothes, putting on her most splendid gown and a high silk headdress.

An hour later, all the people in the castle were running to the courtyard crying, "Our king has come back! After three long years, our king has returned!"

106

The king greeted everyone kindly, but to his queen he said reproachfully, "Did you not receive my message? I laid a long time in prison waiting to be ransomed! Now you greet me lovingly, but it was a young lute player who rescued me and brought me home!"

The queen had expected to tell the king in the privacy of their chamber the reasons for her disguise and perilous journey, for she feared he would be angry that she had not sent the ransom money. But before she could make a suitable reply, a spiteful minister standing nearby said, "Sire, when news of your imprisonment arrived, the queen left the castle and only returned today."

At this the king looked stricken and sorrowful. He turned away to confer with his ministers, for he thought the queen had deserted him in his time of need. The queen returned to her chamber and put on again her travel-stained minstrel cloak and hood. Taking her lute, she slipped down to the castle courtyard where she sang in a sweet clear voice, the verses she had sung in a far off land:

> I sing the captive's longing
> Within his prison wall,
> Of hearts that sigh when none are nigh
> To answer to their call.
>
> And if you hear my singing
> Within your palace, sire,
> Oh give, I pray, this happy day,
> To me my heart's desire.

As soon as the king heard this song he ran out to meet the lute player, took him by the hand, and led him into the castle.

"Here," he cried, "is the boy who released me from my prison. And now, my true friend, I will indeed give you your heart's desire."

"I ask only your trust and love," said she, throwing off the

107

hooded cloak and revealing herself as the queen. "And I beg that you listen to my story."

A cry of astonishment rang through the hall. The king stood amazed, then rushed to embrace her.

"My dear husband," said the queen as she led him to one side, "I did receive your message, but I chose to follow another plan." Then the queen told him all that had troubled her about the ransom plan, and why she thought it the wiser course to rescue the king, instead, through her skill as a lute player.

"Thus," she ended, "you return not to a sorry kingdom of debts and people overburdened with taxes, but to a prosperous land and contented subjects."

Then the king rejoiced in the wisdom and courage of the queen and, in gratitude, proclaimed a seven day feast of celebration throughout the land.

Dorothy Blackley contributed this story to Andrew Lang's *Olive Fairy Book* (1907) with a note that it had a Russian source. However, the story seems to have a general European locale. The idea of minstrel disguise for gaining safe access to a palace or king was used in tales of the thirteenth century. This retelling by the editor somewhat expands Blackley's nineteenth-century story.

CLEVER MANKA

There once was a rich farmer who was as grasping and mean as he was rich. He was always driving a hard bargain and always getting the better of his poor neighbors. One of these neighbors was a humble shepherd to whom the farmer owed payment of a calf. When the time of payment came, the farmer refused to give the shepherd the calf, forcing the shepherd to bring the matter to the burgomaster* of the village.

The burgomaster was a young man who was not very experienced. He listened to both sides, and when he had thought a bit, he said, "Instead of making a decision on this case, I will put a riddle to you both, and the man who makes the best answer shall have the calf. Are you agreed?"

The farmer and the shepherd accepted this proposal, and the burgomaster said, "Well then, here is my riddle: What is the swiftest thing in the world? What is the sweetest thing? What is the richest? Think out your answers and bring them to me at this same time tomorrow."

The farmer went home in a temper. "What kind of a burgomaster is this young fellow!" he growled. "If he had let me keep the calf, I'd have sent him a bushel of pears. Now I may lose the calf, for I can't think of an answer to his foolish riddle."

"What is the riddle?" asked his wife. "Perhaps I can help you." The farmer told her the riddle, and his wife said that of course she knew the answers.

*A burgomaster is the mayor of a village.

109

"Our gray mare must be the swiftest thing in the world," said she. "You know that nothing ever passes us on the road. As for the sweetest, did you ever taste any honey sweeter than ours? And I'm sure there's nothing richer than our chest of golden ducats that we've saved up over the years."

The farmer was delighted. "You're right! Now we will be able to keep the calf!"

Meanwhile, when the shepherd got home, he was very downcast and sad. His daughter, a clever girl named Manka, asked what troubled him.

The shepherd sighed. "I'm afraid I've lost the calf. The burgomaster gave us a riddle to solve, and I know I shall never guess it."

"What is the riddle? Perhaps I can help you," said Manka.

The shepherd told her the riddle, and the next day, as he was setting out for the burgomaster's, Manka told him the answers.

When the shepherd reached the burgomaster's house, the farmer was already there. The burgomaster repeated the riddle and then asked the farmer his answers.

The farmer said with a pompous air: "The swiftest thing in the world? Why that's my gray mare, of course, for no other horse ever passes us on the road. The sweetest? Honey from my beehives. The richest? What can be richer than my chest of gold pieces?"

"Hmmm," said the burgomaster. "And what answers does the shepherd make?"

"The swiftest thing in the world," said the shepherd, "is thought, for thought can run any distance in the twinkling of an eye. The sweetest thing of all is sleep, for when a person is tired and sad, what can be sweeter? The richest thing is the earth, for out of the earth come all the riches of the world."

"Good!" cried the burgomaster. "The calf goes to the shepherd."

Later the burgomaster said to the shepherd, "Tell me now, who gave you those answers? I'm sure you never thought of them yourself."

The shepherd was unwilling to tell, but finally he confessed that the answers came from his daughter Manka. The burgomaster became very interested in the cleverness of Manka, and he sent his housekeeper for ten eggs and gave them to the shepherd.

"Take these eggs to Manka and tell her to have them hatched by tomorrow and bring me the chicks," said he.

The shepherd went home and gave Manka the eggs and the message. Manka laughed and said, "Take a handful of corn and bring it back to the burgomaster with this message, "My daughter says if you plant this corn, grow it, and have it harvested by tomorrow, she will bring you the ten chicks to feed on your ripe grain."

When the burgomaster heard this answer, he laughed heartily. "That's a very clever daughter you have! I'd like to meet her. Tell her to come to see me, but she must come neither by day nor by night, neither riding nor walking, neither dressed nor undressed."

Manka smiled when she received this message. The next dawn, when night was gone and day not yet arrived, she set out. She had wrapped herself in a fishnet, and throwing one leg over a goat's back and keeping one foot on the ground, she went to the burgomaster's house.

Now I ask you, did she go dressed? No, she wasn't dressed, for a fishnet isn't clothing. Did she go undressed? Of course not, for wasn't she covered with a fishnet? Did she walk to the burgomaster's? No, she didn't walk, for she went with one leg thrown over a goat. Then did she ride? Of course she didn't ride, for wasn't she walking on one foot?

When she reached the burgomaster's house, she called out, "Here I am, and I've come neither by day nor by night, neither riding nor walking, neither dressed nor undressed."

The young burgomaster was so delighted with Manka's cleverness that he proposed to her, and in a short time they were married.

"But understand, my dear Manka," he said, "you are not to use your cleverness at my expense. You must not interfere in any of my cases. If you give advice to those who come to me for judgment, I'll send you home to your father!"

"Very well," said Manka. "I agree not to give advice in your cases unless you ask for it."

All went well for a time. Manka was busy with housekeeping, and was careful not to interfere in any of the burgomaster's cases.

Then one day two farmers came to the burgomaster to have a dispute settled. One of the farmers owned a mare which had foaled in the marketplace. The colt had run under the wagon of the other farmer, and the owner of the wagon claimed the colt as his property.

The burgomaster was thinking of something else while the case was being argued, and he said carelessly, "The man who found the colt under his wagon is the owner of the colt."

The farmer who owned the mare met Manka as he was leaving the house, and stopped to tell her about the case. Manka was ashamed that her husband had made so foolish a decision. She said to the farmer, "Come back this afternoon with a fishing net and stretch it across the dusty road. When the burgomaster sees you, he will come out and ask what you are doing. Tell him you are catching fish. When he asks, how you can expect to catch fish in a dusty road, tell him it's just as easy to catch fish in a dusty road as it is for a wagon to foal a colt. . . . He'll see the injustice of his decision and have the colt returned to you. But remember one thing—you must not let him know that I told you to do this."

That afternoon when the burgomaster looked out of his window, he saw a man stretching a fishnet across the dusty road. He went out and asked, "What are you doing?"

"Fishing."

"Fishing in a dusty road? Are you crazy?"

"Well," said the man, "it's just as easy for me to catch fish in a dusty road as it is for a wagon to foal."

Then the burgomaster realized he had made a careless and unjust decision. "Of course, the colt belongs to your mare and it must be returned to you," he said. "But tell me, who put you up to this? You didn't think of it yourself!"

The farmer tried not to tell, but the burgomaster persisted and when he found out that Manka was at the bottom of it he became very angry. He rushed into the house and called his wife.

"Manka," he said, "I told you what would happen if you interfered in any of my cases! I won't hear any excuses. Home you go this very day, and you may take with you the one thing you like best in the house."

Manka did not argue. "Very well, my dear husband. I shall go home to my father's cottage and take with me the one thing I like best in the house. But I will not go until after supper. We have been very happy together, and I should like to eat one last meal with you. Let us have no more angry words, but be kind to each other as we've always been, and then part as friends."

The burgomaster agreed to this, and Manka prepared a fine supper of all the dishes her husband particularly liked. The burgomaster opened his choicest wine and pledged Manka's health. Then he set to eat, and the supper was so good that he ate and ate and ate. And the more he ate, the more he drank, until at last he grew drowsy and fell sound asleep in his chair. Then, without awakening him, Manka had him carried out to the wagon that was waiting to take her home to her father.

The next morning when the burgomaster opened his eyes, he found himself lying in the shepherd's cottage.

"What does this mean?" he roared.

"Nothing, dear husband," said Manka. "You know you told me I might take with me the one thing I liked best in your house, so of course I took you! That's all."

The burgomaster stared at her in amazement. Then he laughed loud and heartily to think how Manka had outwitted him.

"Manka," he said, "you're too clever for me. Come, my dear, let's go home."

So they climbed back into the wagon and drove home.

The burgomaster never again scolded his wife, but after that, whenever a very difficult case came up, he always said, "I think we had better consult my wife. You know she's a very clever woman."

Variations of this Central European story appear in different cultures and countries. "The Innkeeper's Daughter" is an exact parallel in Jewish folklore, while a similar tale, "The Basil Plant," is found in Chile. All folk tales of this type turn on a woman's wise answers, usually to riddles. This retelling by the editor is taken from P. Fillmore's story in *Shoemaker's Apron* (1920).

THE SHEPHERD OF MYDDVAI
AND THE LAKE MAIDEN

Long, long ago in the mountains of Wales, there lived a young shepherd lad with his mother. They lived in the wide sloping valley, and every day the lad drove his flock up through the rocky pass to the fine pasture land surrounding a clear blue lake.

He was a quiet lad given to dreaming as the flocks grazed and fashioning light airy tunes on the reed pipes he carried. It was a simple life, and although his mother sometimes sighed and wished the lad were more ambitious, still they did have a snug cottage and healthy livestock.

One day, at midsummer, the shepherd was resting in the shade and unwrapping the round, hard-baked barley loaf his mother had packed for him. Suddenly three maidens rose up from the waters of the lake, glided to shore, and wandered among the wild flowers. Each had long golden hair and moved with an airy grace that was a joy to behold. One of the maidens came close to where the shepherd lay quite still with wonder. Her face, indeed her whole being, shone with a radiance that was scarcely human.

The lad spoke to her and shyly offered her his bread. The maiden took the loaf and tried it. Then she gave it back and sang,

> Hard, too hard is thy bread;
> That will never feed me.

And she ran off laughing into the waters of the lake.

That evening the lad returned home with his flock and hurried in to tell his mother about the strange and wonderful happening.

"She was that radiant and merry," said the lad at the end, "I fell in love with her. I'll have no other for my wife!"

"'Tis bewitched you are!" said his mother, shaking her head. Then she added briskly, "Your bread was too hard for her, was it? I'll mix up more dough and bake it soft, but I doubt you'll see her again."

Nonetheless the shepherd lad did see her again the very next day. This time the Lake Maiden came forth alone, and in the lad's eyes she shone as radiantly as dew in the morning sun. They walked together by the shore of the lake, and the shepherd told her he loved her. He said he would marry no one but herself.

But when he offered her the soft bread, she tried it, then sang,

> Unbaked is thy bread,
> I will not have thee.

With a mocking laugh the maiden ran lightly back to the waters of the lake and disappeared.

When he returned home with his flock that evening, the lad told his mother the bread was too soft. "Unbaked, she called it," he said in despair.

"We'll try again," said his mother getting out her finest ground flour. And this time she baked a perfect loaf for her son to take with him. It was crisp on the outside, light and well-baked within.

Long and anxiously he waited the next day until he feared she would not come at all. On his reed pipes he played the airy tunes she liked, and then a plaintive melody to tell his heart's longing. Toward evening the maiden rose from the lake and came toward him.

The shepherd hastened to meet her. Humbly he offered the round baked loaf. On an impulse he sprinkled the offering with a few drops of lake water.

The Lake Maiden tasted the bread. Smiling, she said she would leave the lake and dwell with him. Then she raised her arm toward the lake and beckoned. Up from the water rose several sleek cows, a bull, and two oxen. They splashed ashore and stood behind her.

"There is one condition," said she. "You must never touch me with anything made of iron. For if you do, I cannot stay with you no matter how much I may want to. I must return to the lake with my cattle, and you will never see me again."

Joyfully the shepherd agreed. "That will be an easy condition to remember," he answered. "I will never let anything made of iron touch you." Proudly he led home his bride and the herd of fairy cattle.

They lived happily together for many years. Two sons and a daughter were born to them and grew up to be strong, healthy, and wise. In that part of Wales, no one had ever seen so much milk, or tasted such fine butter and cheese as came from the fairy cows. The family had good fortune with all their livestock and became prosperous.

Now as the years passed, the shepherd grew old and gray —but the Lake Maiden never seemed to change. She still had the same radiant appearance as the first day she rose from the waters of the lake.

One day the husband and wife went out to the hillside to catch some ponies, for they planned to ride into market. The wife was still as fleet as a girl, and in a few minutes she had caught a pony by the mane.

"Throw me the halter," she called.

But the husband, without thinking, threw the bridle, and the iron bit struck his wife's hand.

The Lake Maiden let go the pony and stood for a moment looking at him sadly. Then she sang,

> Brindle cow, white speckled,
> Spotted cow, bold freckled;
> Old Whiteface, and gray Berenger,
> The white bull, the gray ox,

And the black calf, come!
All come and follow me home.

The sky grew dark, the wind lashed the trees. The Lake Maiden walked back up the mountain. All the fairy cattle and their offspring followed her—the cows from the byre, the bulls from the pasture, the oxen with the plows still dragging behind them. The Lake Maiden entered the lake, her fairy cattle behind her.

The old shepherd went back to the house and wept. He called in his family and told them all that had happened, for they had never heard the story of their mother before.

The brothers and sister believed their mother might be seen again. Every evening they climbed up the rocky track to watch patiently by the shore of the lake. But the lake was still and calm, week after week, with only a breeze faintly stirring the surface.

At last one evening when the sun was lying low in the west, and all three were watching quietly, the Lake Maiden rose out of the water and came to them.

"I will always love you, and I will always watch over you," she said. "I will watch over your children's children, and those who come after them. This one last time I have come back to teach you all the healing charms."

Then she walked with them through the meadows, showing them where all the healing plants grew: one for eye infections, one for fever, another for healing all wounds. She taught them when and how to gather the plants, how to boil and prepare them.

So much of the art of healing did she teach them before she returned to the lake, that these three became the wisest and the most skilled physicians in Wales. They taught all these things to their daughters and to their sons. In this way the knowledge and the art of healing was passed to their children's children, and to each new generation long into time.

Their extraordinary powers of healing brought fame and

The Lake Maiden entered the lake,
her fairy cattle behind her.

renown to the family, and for hundreds of years people came to the village of Myddvai from all over Wales to be healed. For this was the legacy given to her family and their descendants by the Lake Maiden.

In Wales, the Lake Maiden was once a local goddess, and the physicians of Myddvai came from an actual family, renowned for their medical skill for the six centuries before the family died out in 1743. There are different versions of this tale, but all have basically the same plot. This retelling by the editor is from a story in Joseph Jacobs' *Celtic Fairy Tales.*

THE SEARCH FOR THE
MAGIC LAKE

Long ago there was a ruler of the vast Inca Empire who had an only son. This youth brought great joy to his father's heart but also a sadness, for the prince had been born in ill health.

As the years passed the prince's health did not improve, and none of the court doctors could find a cure for his illness.

One night the aged emperor went down on his knees and prayed at the altar.

"Oh Great Ones," he said, "I am getting older and will soon leave my people and join you in the heavens. There is no one to look after them but my son, the prince. I pray you make him well and strong so he can be a fit ruler for my people. Tell me how his malady can be cured."

The emperor put his head in his hands and waited for an answer. Soon he heard a voice coming from the fire that burned constantly in front of the altar.

"Let the prince drink water from the magic lake at the end of the world," the voice said, "and he will be well."

At that moment the fire sputtered and died. Among the cold ashes lay a golden flask.

But the emperor was much too old to make the long journey to the end of the world, and the young prince was too ill to travel. So the emperor proclaimed that whoever should fill the golden flask with the magic water would be greatly rewarded.

Many brave men set out to search for the magic lake, but none could find it. Days and weeks passed and still the flask remained empty.

In a valley, some distance from the emperor's palace, lived a poor farmer who had a wife, two grown sons, and a young daughter.

One day the older son said to his father, "Let my brother and me join in the search for the magic lake. Before the moon is new again, we shall return and help you harvest the corn and potatoes."

The father remained silent. He was not thinking of the harvest, but feared for his sons' safety.

When the father did not answer, the second son added, "Think of the rich reward, Father!"

"It is their duty to go," said his wife, "for we must all try to help our emperor and the young prince."

After his wife had spoken, the father yielded.

"Go, if you must, but beware of the wild beasts and evil spirits," he cautioned.

With their parents' blessing, and an affectionate farewell from their young sister, the sons set out on their journey.

They found many lakes, but none where the sky touched the water.

Finally the young brother said, "Before another day has passed we must return to help father with the harvest."

"Yes," agreed the other, "but I have thought of a plan. Let us each carry a jar of water from any lake along the way. We can say it will cure the prince. Even if it doesn't, surely the emperor will give us a small reward for our trouble."

"Agreed," said the younger brother.

On arriving at the palace, the youths told the emperor and his court that they brought water from the magic lake. At once the prince was given a sip from each of the brother's jars, but of course he remained as ill as before.

"Perhaps the water must be sipped from the golden flask," one of the high priests said.

But the golden flask would not hold the water. In some mysterious way, the water from the jars disappeared as soon as it was poured into the flask.

In despair the emperor called for his magician and said to him, "Can you break the spell of the flask so the water will remain for my son to drink?"

"I cannot do that, your majesty," replied the magician. "But I believe," he added wisely, "that the flask is telling us that we have been deceived by the two brothers. The flask can be filled only with water from the magic lake."

When the brothers heard this, they trembled with fright, for they knew their falsehood was discovered.

So angry was the emperor that he ordered the brothers thrown into chains. Each day they were forced to drink water from their jars as a reminder of their false deed. News of their disgrace spread far and wide.

Again the emperor sent messengers throughout the land pleading for someone to bring the magic water before death claimed him and the young prince.

Súmac, the little sister of the youths, was tending her flock of llamas when she heard the sound of the royal trumpet. Then came the voice of the emperor's servant with his urgent message from the court.

Quickly the child led her llamas home and begged her parents to let her go in search of the magic water.

"You are too young," her father said. "Besides, look at what has already befallen your brothers. Some evil spirit must have taken hold of them to make them tell such a lie."

And her mother said, "We could not bear to be without our precious Súmac!"

"But think how sad our emperor will be if the young prince dies," replied Súmac. "And if I can find the magic lake, perhaps the emperor will forgive my brothers and send them home."

"Dear husband," said Súmac's mother, "maybe it is the will of the gods that we let her go."

Once again the father gave his permission.

Súmac was overjoyed, and went skipping out to the corral to harness one of her pet llamas. It would carry her provisions and keep her company.

Meanwhile her mother filled a little woven bag with food and drink for Súmac—toasted golden kernels of corn and a little earthen jar of <u>chicha</u>, a beverage made from crushed corn.

The three embraced each other tearfully before Súmac set out bravely on her mission, leading her pet llama along the trail.

The first night she slept, snug and warm against her llama, in the shelter of a few rocks. But when she heard the hungry cry of the puma, she feared for her pet animal and bade it return safely home.

The next night she spent in the top branches of a tall tree, far out of reach of the dreadful puma. She hid her provisions in a hole in the tree trunk.

At sunrise she was aroused by the voices of gentle sparrows resting on a nearby limb.

"Poor child," said the oldest sparrow, "she can never find her way to the lake."

"Let us help her," chorused the others.

"Oh please do!" implored the child, "and forgive me for intruding in your tree."

"We welcome you," chirped another sparrow, "for you are the same little girl who yesterday shared your golden corn with us."

"We shall help you," continued the first sparrow, who was the leader, "for you are a good child. Each of us will give you a wing feather, and you must hold them all together in one hand as a fan. The feathers have magic powers that will carry you wherever you wish to go. They will also protect you from harm."

Each sparrow then lifted a wing, sought out a special feather hidden underneath, and gave it to Súmac. She fashioned them into the shape of a little fan, taking the ribbon from her

124

hair to bind the feathers together so that none would be lost.

"I must warn you," said the oldest sparrow, "that the lake is guarded by three terrible creatures. But have no fear. Hold the magic fan up to your face and you will be unharmed."

Súmac thanked the birds over and over again. Then, holding up the fan in her hands she said politely, "Please magic fan, take me to the lake at the end of the world."

A soft breeze swept her out of the top branches of the tree and through the valley. Then up she was carried, higher and higher into the sky, until she could look down and see the great mountain peaks covered with snow.

At last the wind put her down on the shore of a beautiful lake. It was, indeed, the lake at the end of the world, for, on the opposite side from where she stood, the sky came down so low it touched the water.

Súmac tucked the magic fan into her waistband and ran to the edge of the water. Suddenly her face fell. She had left everything back in the forest. What could she use for carrying the precious water back to the prince?

"Oh, I do wish I had remembered the jar!" she said.

Suddenly she heard a soft thud in the sand at her feet. She looked down and discovered a beautiful golden flask—the same one the emperor had found in the ashes.

Súmac took the flask and kneeled at the water's edge. Just then a hissing voice behind her said, "Get away from my lake or I shall wrap my long, hairy legs around your neck."

Súmac turned around. There stood a giant crab as large as a pig and as black as night.

With trembling hands the child took the magic fan from her waistband and spread it open in front of her face. As soon as the crab looked at it, he closed his eyes and fell down on the sand in a deep sleep.

Once more Súmac started to fill the flask. This time she was startled by a fierce voice bubbling up from the water.

"Get away from my lake or I shall eat you," gurgled a giant green alligator. His long tail beat the water angrily.

Súmac waited until the creature swam closer. Then she

held up the fan. The alligator blinked. He drew back. Slowly, quietly, he sank to the bottom of the lake in a sound sleep.

Before Súmac could recover from her fright, she heard a shrill whistle in the air. She looked up and saw a flying serpent. His skin was red as blood. Sparks flew from his eyes.

"Get away from my lake or I shall bite you," hissed the serpent as it batted its wings around her head.

Again Súmac's fan saved her from harm. The serpent closed his eyes and drifted to the ground. He folded his wings and coiled up on the sand. Then he began to snore.

Súmac sat for a moment to quiet herself. Then, realizing that the danger was past, she sighed with great relief.

"Now I can fill the golden flask and be on my way," she said to herself.

When this was done, she held the flask tightly in one hand and clutched the fan in the other.

"Please take me to the palace," she said.

Hardly were the words spoken, when she found herself safely in front of the palace gates. She looked at the tall guard.

"I wish to see the emperor," Súmac uttered in trembling tones.

"Why, little girl?" the guard asked kindly.

"I bring water from the magic lake to cure the prince."

The guard looked down at her in astonishment.

"Come!" he commanded in a voice loud and deep as thunder.

In just a few moments Súmac was led into a room full of sadness. The emperor was pacing up and down in despair. The prince lay motionless on a huge bed. His eyes were closed and his face was without color. Beside him knelt his mother, weeping.

Without wasting words, Súmac went to the prince and gave him a few drops of magic water. Soon he opened his eyes. His cheeks became flushed. It was not long before he sat up in bed. He drank some more.

"How strong I feel!" the prince cried joyfully.

The emperor and his wife embraced Súmac. Then Súmac

told them of her adventurous trip to the lake. They praised her courage. They marveled at the reappearance of the golden flask and at the powers of the magic fan.

"Dear child," said the emperor, "all the riches of my empire are not enough to repay you for saving my son's life. Ask what you will and it shall be yours."

"Oh, generous emperor," said Súmac timidly, "I have but three wishes."

"Name them and they shall be yours," urged the emperor.

"First, I wish my brothers to be free to return to my parents. They have learned their lesson and will never be false again. I know they were only thinking of a reward for my parents. Please forgive them."

"Guards, free them at once!" ordered the emperor.

"Secondly, I wish the magic fan returned to the forest so the sparrows may have their feathers again."

This time the emperor had no time to speak. Before anyone in the room could utter a sound, the magic fan lifted itself up, spread itself wide open, and floated out the window toward the woods. Everyone watched in amazement. When the fan was out of sight, they applauded.

"What is your last wish, dear Súmac?" asked the queen mother.

"I wish that my parents be given a large farm and great flocks of llamas, vicuñas, and alpacas, so they will not be poor any longer."

"It will be so," said the emperor, "but I am sure your parents never considered themselves poor with so wonderful a daughter."

"Won't you stay with us in the palace?" ventured the prince.

"Yes, stay with us!" urged his father and mother. "We will do everything to make you happy."

"Oh thank you," said Súmac happily, "but I must return to my parents and my brothers. I miss them as I know they have missed me. They do not even know I am safe, for I came directly to your palace."

The royal family did not try to detain Súmac any longer.

"My own guard will see that you get home safely," said the emperor.

When she reached home, she found that all she had wished for had come to pass: her brothers were waiting for her with their parents; a beautiful house and huge barn were being constructed; her father had received a deed granting him many acres of new, rich farm land.

Súmac ran into the arms of her happy family.

This tale is reprinted from Genevieve Barlow's *Latin American Tales* (1966) and was told to the author by Incas living in Ecuador. The Inca Empire extended over Ecuador, Peru, and Bolivia from the twelfth to the sixteenth centuries.

THE SQUIRE'S BRIDE

There was once a very rich squire who owned a large farm, had plenty of silver in his money chest, and gold in the bank, but there was something he had not, and that was a wife.

One day a neighbor's daughter was working for the squire in the hayfield. He liked her very much, and as she was a poor farmer's daughter, the squire thought that if he only mentioned marriage she would be more than glad to accept at once.

So he said to her, "I've been thinking I want to marry."

"Well, one may think of many things," said the lassie as she stood there. She really thought the old fellow ought to be thinking of something that suited him better than getting married to a young lass at his time of life.

"I was thinking that you should be my wife!" said he.

"No, thank you," said she, "and much obliged for the honor."

The squire was not used to being refused, and the more she refused him, the more he wanted her. But the lassie would not listen to him at all. So the old squire sent for her father. He told the farmer to talk to his daughter and arrange the marriage. Then the squire would forgive the farmer the money he had lent him and would give him the piece of land which lay close to his meadow in the bargain.

"Yes, yes, be sure I'll bring the lass to her senses," said the father. "She is young and does not know what is best for her."

But all his coaxing, all his threats, and all his talking went for naught. She said she would not have the old miser, if he sat buried in gold up to his ears.

The squire waited and waited, but at last he got angry. The next day he visited the poor farmer and told him that he had to settle the matter at once if he expected the squire to stand by his bargain. For now he would wait no longer to be married.

The farmer knew no other way out, but to agree to let the squire get everything ready for the wedding. Then when the parson and the wedding guests had arrived, the squire would send for the lassie as if she were wanted for some work.

When she reached him, the squire thought, she would be so awed by the fine bridal clothes and the wedding guests that she would agree to be married, for he could not believe a farm girl would really refuse a rich husband.

When the guests had arrived, the squire called one of his farm lads and told him to run down to his neighbor to ask him to send up immediately what he had promised.

"But if you are not back with her in a twinkling," he said, shaking his fist at him, "I'll. . ."

He did not finish, for the lad ran off as if he had been shot at from behind.

"My master has sent me to ask for that which you promised him," said the lad, when he got to the neighbor. "But pray, lose no time, for master is terribly busy today."

"Yes, yes, run down in the meadow and take her with you," answered the girl's father.

The lad ran off and when he came to the meadow, he found the daughter raking hay.

"I am to fetch what your father has promised my master," said the lad.

"Aha!" thought she. "Is that what they are up to?" And with a twinkle in her eye she said, "Oh yes, it's that little bay mare of ours, I suppose. You had better go and take her. She stands grazing on the other side of the pea field."

The boy jumped on the back of the horse and rode her home at a full gallop.

"Have you got her with you?" asked the squire.

"She is down at the door," said the lad.

"Take her up to the room my mother had," said the squire.

"But master, how can I?" said the lad.

"Do as I tell you!" roared the old squire. "And if <u>you</u> can't persuade her, get someone to help you!"

When the lad saw his master's face, he knew it would be no use to argue. So he went and got all the farm hands together to help him. Some pulled at the head of the mare, and others pushed from behind, and at last they got her upstairs and into the room where they tied the reins to a bedpost. The wedding finery, with the crown and flowered wreath, was spread out on the bed all ready for the bride.

"Well, that's done, master," said the lad when he returned. He mopped his brow. "That was the hardest job I've ever had here on the farm."

"Never mind, never mind, you shall not have done it for nothing," said the master. He pulled a silver coin out of his pocket and gave it to the lad. "Now send the women up to dress her."

"But, I say, master. How can they?"

"None of your talk," cried the squire. "Tell them to dress her in the wedding clothes, and mind not to forget either wreath or crown!"

The lad ran into the kitchen. "Listen here, lasses," he called out. "The master's gone daft! You are to go upstairs and dress up the bay mare as a bride. I suppose he wants to play a joke on his guests!"

The women laughed and laughed, but ran upstairs and dressed the horse in all the finery that was there. And then the lad went and told his master that now all was ready, complete with wreath and crown.

"Very well, bring her down. I will meet her at the door myself," said the squire.

There was a loud clatter and thumping on the stairs as the mare was led down. Then the door was thrown open to the large room where the squire waited with the wedding guests.

In walked the bay mare dressed as a bride, with a wreath of flowers falling over one eye. The parson gaped in astonishment. The guests broke into loud laughter, and as for the squire—they say he never went courting again.

Norwegian folk tales often have an earthy humor. Gudrun Thorne-Thomsen's translation (1912) is the source for this retelling by the editor.

WILD GOOSE LAKE

Long ago in China, a young girl lived in a small village at the foot of Horse Ear Mountain. Her name was Sea Girl and she lived with her father, a hard-working farmer.

No rain had fallen for many months; the crops hung limp and brown, dying for want of water. It seemed there could be no harvest, and food was already scarce. So each day Sea Girl went up on Horse Ear Mountain and cut bamboo to make brooms to sell.

One day when Sea Girl had climbed higher on the mountain than ever before in her search for bamboo, she saw a large blue lake gleaming in the sun. The water of the lake was clear and still. Not a single fallen leaf marred its surface, for whenever a leaf fell from the trees surrounding the lake, a large wild goose flew down and carried it away. This was the Wild Goose Lake Sea Girl had heard the elders speak of in the village tales.

Sea Girl carried her bamboo home, thinking of the clear blue water of the lake and how badly the people needed water for their crops.

The next day she took her axe to cut bamboo and again climbed high in the mountain. She hoped she could make an outlet from Wild Goose Lake. The village harvest would be saved if the lake water trickled down the mountain in a gentle stream to the farms below.

She began to walk around the lake, following the narrow sandy shore. But the lake was surrounded by jagged rocks, high cliffs, and dense forest. There seemed to be no place to make an outlet for a stream. Then late in the day, she came up-on a thick stone gate. Her axe was of no help, and although she used all her strength, the gate could not be moved.

Wearily she dropped her pile of bamboo cuttings and sat down next to the gate. All was still, and the lake was a mirror reflecting the dark green pines. A wild goose swooped high in the sky, then glided down to stand on the ground nearby.

"Sea Girl," said the Wild Goose, "you will need the Golden Key to open the gate."

Before she could ask where she could find the Golden Key, the wild goose spread her wings and soared away over the lake. Then Sea Girl noticed a small keyhole in the stone gate, but there was no key.

Sea Girl walked on along the shore of the lake, searching for the Golden Key. She came to a forest of cypress trees and sitting on a cypress branch was a brilliant parrot of scarlet and green.

"Parrot," she called, "do you know where I can find the Golden Key that will open the stone gate?"

The parrot answered, "You must first find the third daugh-ter of the Dragon King, for the Dragon King guards the Golden Key to Wild Goose Lake." With a quick whirring of wings the parrot flew off into the forest.

Sea Girl walked on searching for the Dragon King's third daughter. In a pine grove close to the lake, she saw a peacock sitting on a low branch.

"Peacock, peacock," she called, "where can I find the Dragon King's third daughter?"

"The Dragon King's third daughter loves songs. If you sing the songs your village people sing, she will come forth from the lake." The peacock dropped a feather at her feet and flew away.

Sea Girl picked up the feather and began to sing. Her voice was clear, and as fresh as a lark's song. At first she sang about the snowflakes drifting on the mountains, but the Dragon King's third daughter did not appear. She sang of green reeds bending in the wind. Still the third daughter did not come; the

"We will sing to the eagle,"
said Sea Girl.

lake lay clear and still. Then Sea Girl sang of pale blossoming flowers on the hills.

Near the shore the water broke into a glittering spray, and the third daughter came up out of the lake to stand before Sea Girl.

"Deep in the lake I heard your songs," she said. "They are so strange and beautiful that I could not resist them. My father does not allow us to meet humans, but I have come to you secretly. I, too, love songs, and your songs are finer than mine."

Sea Girl asked, "Are you the third daughter of the Dragon King?"

"Yes, I am Third Daughter. My father and his people guard Wild Goose Lake. Who are you? Why do you sing your songs here?"

"I am Sea Girl. I live in a village at the foot of Horse Ear Mountain, and I have come all this long way to find the Golden Key which opens the stone gate of the lake. The people in my village are hungry and need water to save their harvest."

Third Daughter hesitated, then she said, "I would like to help you. The Golden Key is kept in my father's treasure room, deep in a rock cave. Outside on the cliff a huge eagle guards it, and he would tear to pieces anyone who tried to enter." She pointed to a rock cliff a little distance off. On the cliff perched an eagle nodding in the sun.

Sea Girl asked, "Would your father give us the Golden Key?"

"He will not help humans," sighed Third Daughter. "That is why he had the stone gate made to keep in the lake water. You must wait until my father leaves his palace and goes off. Then perhaps we can lure the eagle away from the treasure room."

So Sea Girl made a bed of soft pine branches under the trees and Third Daughter brought her fresh fish to eat.

A few days later she said to Sea Girl, "My father has left his palace. Now is the time to search for the key, but I don't know how you will slip past the eagle."

"We will sing to him," said Sea Girl.

The two girls moved lightly and quietly closer to where the eagle perched high on the rock cliff. Third Daughter pointed out the entrance to the cave below. Tall ferns and reeds hid the girls from sight, and they began to sing. Each took turns singing the loveliest and most enchanting songs they knew.

At first the eagle just peered around curiously. Then, drawn by the strange haunting sounds, he moved down from the cliff in search of the source. Third Daughter crept quietly further and further away, and the eagle followed the enchanting sound of her voice.

Sea Girl slipped into the treasure cave to search for the Golden Key. At first her eyes were dazzled, for the room was filled on all sides with gold, silver, and sparkling jewels. But Sea Girl did not touch the treasure. She searched only for the Golden Key.

Just as she was about to give up in despair, she saw a small plain wooden box sitting on a shelf in the corner. Quickly she opened it and peered in. There lay the gleaming Golden Key!

Sea Girl took the key and returned to where Third Daughter waited. When the delicate soaring melody of song ceased, the eagle shook himself, spread his wings, and sailed back to his cliff.

Then Sea Girl and Third Daughter hastened back to the stone gate. The Golden Key fit perfectly into the keyhole, and the gate swung open. At once the water rushed out in a leaping cascade, down the mountainside to the village. In a very short time all the canals and ditches of the farms were full and overflowing with water.

Third Daughter saw that the village would soon be flooded and she called out, "Sea Girl, Sea Girl, there is too much water. The crops will be washed away and lost!"

Sea Girl quickly threw in the piles of bamboo she had left earlier at the stone gate. But that slowed the water only a little. Then the two girls rolled boulders and large rocks into the stream until the water slowed down to a small bubbling brook. Now they knew the village would always have a steady supply of water.

When the Dragon King returned and found the Golden Key was gone, he was very angry. He banished Third Daughter from the palace. But Third Daughter went to live very happily with Sea Girl, and they sang their songs together as they worked.

So beautiful were their songs that each year ever after, on the twenty-second day of the seventh moon, all the women of the surrounding villages came together to sing the songs they knew and to celebrate the heroic deed of Sea Girl.

This version was adapted by the editor from a tale in *Folk Tales of China* (1965), edited by Wolfram Eberhard. The story is not, in fact, "Chinese," but comes from a minority group living in southwest China, the *I* tribes of Yun-nan. However, the dragon king is frequently found in Chinese tales, and the importance given to folksinging is typical of many groups in southern and western China.

BUCCA DHU AND BUCCA GWIDDEN

You must know that there are two buccas. Bucca Dhu is the bad goblin, and Bucca Gwidden is the good one. But Bucca Dhu is much bigger and stronger and fiercer than Bucca Gwidden, who is but a little meek thing, after all.

Now once upon a time there was a gay old woman who lived on a farm with her son and her daughter-in-law. The old woman was very fond of playing cards, and even of dancing and singing, though the son and the daughter-in-law thought she ought to know better at her time of life. Wherever people were gathered together to enjoy themselves, there the old woman would be: if it was card-playing, she would fling down her pennies and play with the rest; if it was dancing, she would tuck up her petticoats and foot it right merrily; and if it was singing, she would bawl away in her cracked voice, till she had everyone laughing.

When these parties were over and she set out to walk back to the farm, she would call at the inn on her way, and take a glass or two of hot toddy to keep out the cold, and that made her sing all the louder. And so she would wander home, through dark night or clear night, or wet night or fine night, with her bonnet over one eye and her shawl trailing, and as merry as a cricket in the hedge.

The son didn't like it, nor yet did the daughter-in-law, for they were very proper sort of people.

"She puts us to shame," they said.

139

So they decided to give her such a fright that she would never venture out at night again.

One dark night, the daughter-in-law fetched a big sheet and put it over the son's head, and tied it round his neck and wrists. He couldn't see very well inside the sheet, so she took him by the hand and led him to a stile that the old woman had to pass over.

"Stay here by the brush," said the daughter-in-law, "and when your mother clambers up on to the top of the stile, jump out and wave your arms and groan. That'll scare her! She won't want to go over that stile at night again in a hurry!"

And she went back to the farm, and left him standing under the bush.

He waited a long time. It was a windy night, and the bush creaked and rustled and waved its branches about. The man soon began to wish himself safe home again. It seemed to him that there was something alive behind him in the bush, and he kept turning round, but he couldn't see with the sheet over his head. The more the bush creaked and rustled, the more certain he became that there was something lurking there, and he began to think of all the tales he had heard about the bad Bucca Dhu, with his long claws to scratch with, and his great teeth to bite with, for it was just the kind of night when goblins are abroad.

Every minute that passed, the man was getting more and more fearful, and still there was no sign of the old woman. But at last he heard her coming along the path beyond the stile, hopping from one foot to the other, and singing,

> On this black night there's nought to see
> But Bucca Dhu and me, and me!

"Now keep thy distance, Bucca Dhu," she called over her shoulder. "I aren't afraid of 'ee!"

And so she scrambled up on the top of the stile.

When her son heard her speaking to Bucca Dhu, his teeth began to chatter, but he leaped out from the bush, and waved

140

his arms inside the sheet, and groaned, just as the daughter-in-law had told him to do.

The old woman sat down on the stile and laughed.

"Well now," says she, "if it ain't good little Bucca Gwidden! But thou'st best run along home, my dear, for that old Bucca Dhu is a-following of me close, and if he catches thee, he'll tear thy eyes out!...Here he is, here he is! she cried, turning to looking back over the stile. "He's getting bigger every minute, and he's in some rage! Run, Bucca Gwidden, run, run for thy life!"

Her son didn't wait to be told twice. He gathered up the sheet about his knees as well as he could, and he ran. And since he couldn't see where he was going, he bumped into trees, and stumbled over stones, and fell down, and scrambled up again, and stumbled again.

The old woman sat on the top of the stile and kicked with her heels and clapped with her hands.

"Run, Bucca Gwidden, run, run, run!" she screamed. "After him, Bucca Dhu, catch him, boy, catch him! Well run, Bucca Gwidden, well run Bucca Dhu! Tear him, Bucca Dhu! Run, Bucca Gwidden!"

When the briars caught the sheet, the son thought it was Bucca Dhu's claws were in him, and when he ran against the branches of a tree, he thought it was Bucca Dhu's arms were round him; and all the while he ran, the old woman sat on the top of the stile and screamed for joy. He got home at last, more dead than alive, and the daughter-in-law had just taken the sheet off him, and sat him down before the fire to catch his breath, when the old woman walked in.

"Oh my, oh my, oh my!" says she. "<u>Such</u> goings on! I met with Bucca Dhu along the way; and we hadn't gone far together when out from a bush leaps Bucca Gwidden! And that great big bucca he set on the little bucca and chased him for his life! One ran, and t'other ran, and 'twas the merriest chase that ever I did see!"

"I can't tell 'ee if Bucca Dhu catched Bucca Gwidden—

maybe he did, and maybe he didn't. Nor I can't exactly tell 'ee what Bucca Dhu was dressed in. But sure as I'm alive, Bucca Gwidden was wearing one of our sheets; and believe it or not, son, he had boots on just like thine!"

The son smirked, and the daughter-in-law looked foolish. They saw that the old woman was too clever for them, and they never tried to interfere with her again. So she lived merrily all her days.

"Buccas" are mischievous spirits found in the folklore of Cornwall, but they are similar to the "poukas" of Ireland and to the pixies and hobgoblins found in other parts of England. The original source for this tale is W. Bottrell's nine-teenth-century collection of Cornish folk tales. The version used here is from *Peter and the Piskies* (1958) by Ruth Manning-Sanders.

THE ENCHANTED BUCK

Lungile sat in the sunshine watching her mother put the finishing stitches in her sedwaba. It was a great occasion, for the sedwaba is the full skirt of black ox skins which no girl wears till her bridal morning. As it takes a long time to make, Lungile's father had prepared the skins many months ago. He had dyed them inky-black with charcoal, till they looked quite like velvet. Then Lungile's mother shaped the skirt to fit tightly round Lungile's waist and fall into soft folds at her knee, and stitched all the pieces together most beautifully. Now the skirt was ready, and Lungile might set out for the home of her betrothed as soon as she pleased.

That evening she saw all the young women who were to accompany her to the wedding, and arranged the day they were to leave. It was kept a deep secret; Lungile's mother and father would not expect to know, for every bride loves to slip away in the early morning without farewells.

Two days later, at the first flush of day, Lungile and her friends set out on their journey. It was early summer; the valleys and hills were covered with thousands of flowers, vivid scarlet or blue like the sky. The air was fresh and crystal clear, and the girls laughed and sang songs of travel. Lungile was full of joy, for her bridegroom was a chief's son, and she had chosen him out of many suitors. She was as cheerful and capable as she was lovely, and many young men had asked her to marry. She tilled the family's land, wove fine reed fences, and the beer she made was the best for miles around; there was no kraal where she would not have been welcome.

The girls journeyed together for some days, till at last they reached the bridegroom's land and went straight to his parents' kraal. His mother greeted them with every kindness, and showed them to a beautiful hut where they would stay till the day of the marriage. They had been expected for some time, and now every man and woman in the village was kept busy with the marriage preparations.

While the women ground corn or went out to gather wood, the bridegroom and his father considered what oxen should be killed for the feast.

"We will take two of those the Chief Maginde sent to me as your sister's marriage gift," said the father. "They are the finest in the herd, but my eldest son and his bride deserve the best."

The first ox was driven up and killed with much ceremony. When all was ready for cooking, and the guests already nearing the kraal, the meat was cut into long strips and set on the fire to roast. As the bridegroom's mother watched in horror, the meat began to jump about on the fire. It simply would not stay in place, and after trying to make it lie still twice, she became frightened.

"There must be witchcraft here!" said she and hurried to call her husband to see this strange thing. She had left the strips of meat on the fire, but when she returned with all the family and guests at her heels, not a bit of the meat remained. All of it had disappeared.

"The animal was bewitched!" cried the father. Everyone looked at the bride's hut. She was a stranger and they suspected her.

"Bring the white bull," said the father. "He is the finest we have. Perhaps if we kill him it may break the spell."

The white bull was brought forward, the most splendid of all the cattle the bridegroom's father had received from Chief Maginde two years before. He was snow-white from head to tail, save for two long, black horns of great beauty.

The bull was killed and the meat cut up. This time it was placed in large pots to boil. All stood by and watched; even the bride had heard of the trouble and waited anxiously in her hut, for witchcraft at her marriage was indeed a misfortune.

For a while all seemed quiet. Then the water began to boil in the pot in which the bull's head had been placed. Instantly there leaped out of the pot a fine young man, with a bearing like that of a great chief. He ran away with incredible speed, and even as he ran he changed into a handsome buck with large antlers. In a moment he was out of sight.

"Bring the bride here," said the Chief. "Without doubt, she is a witch and has brought trouble on us all."

In a few minutes Lungile was brought from her hut with her maids.

"Go back home," shouted the Chief, "and never let us see your face again! You are not the wife for my son, nor would any decent family want you. I send you back to your parents and demand the return of my marriage gift of cattle."

"I am innocent of all harm," cried Lungile. "I have cast no spells and wish no evil to anyone."

"Go away! Go back to your village," shouted all the people there. "You have brought witchcraft here!"

Then they drove her out quickly; she did not further attempt to prove her innocence, but traveled home with her attendants in bitter anger.

Her father and mother were horrified when they heard of her treatment. They did not for a moment believe their daughter was a witch. The marriage gift was returned, and Lungile took her old place in the kraal again and worked as she had before. Only no more suitors came, for no one quite liked the story of the white ox with the black horns. It looked as if the skirt of black ox skins might never be worn.

More than a year went by, and Lungile gradually forgot her troubles. One day in autumn she went out to gather dried mealie-stalks. The air was cool, the sun shone brightly over the great plains, and she sang gaily as she walked along the narrow path. Just as she was about to turn off toward the fields, a beautiful buck came in sight. To her surprise it did not run away, but circled round her, running across the path and slipping in and out of the bushes. She thought she recognized him.

"Where have I seen this handsome animal before?" she said to herself and thought a minute. "Why it is the very same buck that jumped out of the pot at my marriage feast!"

For a moment she felt sad, then she threw back her head and laughed. "Now he will be caught. It is many days since we had meat. I will try to catch him as he passes."

The buck continued to dance around her, coming nearer and nearer, but always just slipping out of her reach. They had left the village lands behind and were drawing nearer to the mountains. She followed till they came to a stream which flowed down a green valley. There the buck stopped to drink, and Lungile jumped forward and seized him by the horns. He did not seem to mind, and drew her with him on a path which ran up the valley near the stream. Lungile found the buck was far stronger than she expected. She could not turn him back, and she would not let him go.

The valley was empty and wild. High waving grass surrounded her. As they went on, a huge forest came into view which covered the lower slopes of a mountain. A blue shadow began to creep across the valley. Lungile saw it and thought, "I shall hardly reach home before dark. The buck is too strong for me; I must give him up."

She let him go with a sigh, and hurried back to reach the plains again before sundown. She had not gone far when she turned her head to see if the buck were still in sight. To her surprise he was following her. She stood still, and in a few minutes the buck was at her side.

"What do you want?" asked Lungile.

The buck only looked at her with his great brown eyes and said nothing. Lungile spoke again. She was sorry for the buck and felt sure that he was in trouble.

This time the buck answered in a soft, low voice, "Follow me to the forest yonder."

"I will come," said Lungile, and turned once more to the great mountain and the forest at its foot.

Before long they reached the first great trees, and there at the entrance to the forest they saw a sight which made Lungile cry out in terror. A huge ogre seated on a wolf was staring at them. Round his forehead he wore a string of animals' eyes which made him look even more horrible. Lungile turned to run, but the buck said to her calmly, "Come, and you will see what I can do," and he walked straight toward the ogre.

The girl followed, but shivered as she heard the ogre say to the buck, "Ha! You will make a fine meal for the wolf, and that young girl will be my dinner!"

Then he stretched out his long arms and leaped forward to catch the buck. The buck did not move; but the instant the ogre's arms touched him, the buck changed into a powerful young man with a spear. The wolf ran off, frightened, into the bush. The ogre, taken by surprise, was slain with the spear.

The young man took the string of animals' eyes from the slain monster's head and threw them on the ground. Instantly they became living bucks. They all looked at the man with great affection and waited for his command.

The young man then turned to Lungile and said, "Will you be kind to these animals and help them? Remember I, too, was a buck."

Lungile nodded, and the young man went on. "Stay here for a few days and do this for me. Gather greens every morning at sunrise and chant this magic song:

> Once my true love was a buck;
> Once my true love was a buck;
> Now he is changed to a strong young man.
> Now bucks, Oh bucks,
> Change, change, and become young men."

"I will do this," said Lungile with admiration in her eyes. "But tell me, are you the white ox who was killed at the marriage feast? And who are these bucks I will sing to?"

"I am that same white ox," said the young man. "I am a great Chief. Because my lands were better than Chief Maginde's and because I had finer cattle and stronger people, he hated me. One day he bewitched me and turned me into a white ox, and said that all my people should be deer. None should be free till I could change my form and become once more a man. He sent me as a marriage gift to the father of your betrothed—and so I came to be killed. You lost your first lover through me, but do not grieve. You will be loved and honored if you will be my bride."

Lungile consented with great joy. She stayed at the edge of the forest for many days. Every morning at sunrise, she rose when the dew was still heavy, and sang the magic song as she gathered the green leaves up and down the hillside. And every day, more and more bucks came down from the mountains and clustered in the forest. They brought with them the does and the small fawns, and in seven days many thousand had gathered together. Then one morning as she sang the magic song, they all changed at the sunrise into men, women, and children.

This was how the enchanted buck regained his people and won a kind, courageous bride. Proudly, he returned with Lungile to her village. The marriage gift he gave to her parents was magnificent, and Lungile married the young Chief amid much rejoicing.

The blacks of southern Africa were known for their complex social organization. This tale, retold by the editor, is from *Fairy Tales from South Africa* (1910) by Sarah F. Bourhill and Beatrice L. Drake, and was told to the authors by South African black women.

MASTERMAID

Once upon a time there was a king who had several sons. The youngest son grew restless at home and wanted to go out into the world to seek adventures. His father tried to dissuade him, but it was no use.

"Very well," said the king as he gave him his blessing. "You'll always find a welcome here when you return."

After the young prince had traveled for some days he came to a giant's house and knocked on the door. The giant was very pleased to see him. He said he could certainly use the services of a young man who was strong and willing. So the prince was given dinner and a room over the stable.

The next morning the giant prepared to take his herd of goats out to pasture. Before he left he said, "You'll find me an easy master if you do as you're told. Today your task is to clean out the stable while I'm away. But you must not go into any of the rooms off the main hall or I will kill you."

So naturally, as soon as the giant went off with the goats, the prince became curious to see the forbidden rooms. The first two rooms contained large pots and various strange objects, but the third room contained a handsome bright-eyed young woman.

"Well!" she said in surprise. "What are you doing here?"

"I've left my father's castle to seek adventure," said the prince, "and the giant has very kindly taken me into his service."

"You may regret it," said she.

"'Tis easy work," said the prince cheerfully. "All I have to do today is clean out the stable."

149

"Yes, but how will you do it? For every shovelful of dung you toss out of the stable, ten more will appear. But I will tell you how to succeed. You must turn the shovel around and toss with the handle; then all the dung will fly out by itself."

"That sounds easy," said he. So he stretched himself out comfortably and talked all day with Maj (for that was her name) of this and that, and they became good friends.

In the later afternoon he went to the stable. First he tried using the shovel the usual way. The more he shoveled the faster the pile of dung grew. So he hastily reversed the shovel as he had been told, and the dung flew out the door. In a trice the stable was clean.

That evening the giant returned. "Have you cleaned out the stable?"

"Yes indeed, master."

When the giant saw the clean stable, he growled, "You must have been talking to Mastermaid."

"Mastermaid? What is that?" said the prince, pretending to look very stupid. "I did it myself the way we did it at home."

The next day before the giant set off again with his herd, he told the lad his task was to fetch home his horse from the hillside. Again he warned him not to enter any other rooms of the house.

As soon as the giant was gone the prince went to visit his friend Maj, the Mastermaid.

"An easy job today," he told her. "I've only to fetch his horse from the hillside. I fancy I can handle him no matter how fresh or skittery he may be."

"It's not as easy as you think," she warned. "Fire and flames will come out of the nostrils of the horse as soon as you near it. But I've discovered some of the giant's magic and I'll tell you what to do. Take the bit that hangs behind the door there and throw it right into the horse's mouth. Then he'll become tame."

So again the prince sat down to talk with Maj the Mastermaid, and a very agreeable day they had. Maj told him she had been captured and kept prisoner by the giant but had been using her wits to learn some of the giant's magic spells. Giants, she said, were really not very clever.

"I'm not either," said the prince sadly.

"No matter," said Maj affectionately. "You have a warm heart and cheerful courage—that is what counts. You never seem to worry," she sighed. "I wish I could be so merry and lighthearted!"

"Aye, but it is your cleverness and wisdom that's saved me from the giant's vengeance!"

From this exchange you can guess that Maj and the prince were falling in love, and they spent the rest of the day talking of how happy they could be together if only they could escape the giant. The day passed so quickly that the prince had quite forgotten the horse until Maj reminded him of it when evening drew near.

Off he went with the magic bit, and, sure enough, the horse spewed out fiery flames as soon as the prince approached him. The prince threw the metal bit into the flames, and the horse became as quiet as a lamb. So the prince rode him home and waited for the giant.

When the giant saw the horse standing quietly in the stable, he roared, "You never did this task by yourself! You've been talking to Mastermaid!"

"Not me," said the prince, all innocence. "I'd like to see this mastermaid you talk of."

On the third day before the giant went off with his herd, he said, "Today you must go to the devil and fetch me my fire tax."

The prince whistled cheerfully as he went in to see Maj. He was confident that she would know how to deal with this task. "You must help me again," said he. "I've never been to the devil. I don't know the way nor how much to collect."

"Listen carefully and I will tell you," said Maj. "Go to the steep rock on the hillside, take the club lying there, and hit the rock three times. Out will come a creature glowing red, with sparks of fire darting from his eyes. Tell him your errand and when he asks how much gold, be sure to say 'Only as much as I can carry.' If you do not say that, he will give you nothing."

151

The prince gave Maj a hug and said, "Och, without you I'd be mincemeat by now! But let's forget that and talk of other things." So he entertained Maj with light talk until soon she was laughing merrily and the day again passed quickly. Finally Maj warned him it was growing late, and it was time to collect the fire tax.

The prince climbed up the hillside to the rock and all happened as Maj had said. The fiery creature grumbled that the prince was lucky to know the right answer, but he gave him as much gold and silver as he could carry. He brought it back to the giant's house, singing gaily as he went.

"Where's my money from the devil?" demanded the giant as soon as he returned.

"It's there on the bench," said the prince.

"Now I'm sure you've been talking to Mastermaid," roared the giant. "I told you I'd wring your neck!"

"Mastermaid, indeed!" said the prince airily. "I wish I knew what it is. It must be a joke."

"You'll know tomorrow," snarled the giant.

The next day he took the prince into the Mastermaid's room and said to her, "Cut him up and boil him in that big pot for my dinner!" Then he went into the other room and fell asleep.

Taking all the old rags, shoes, and rubbish she could find, Maj put it into the large pot with water. "Let the giant sup on that!" said she. Then she picked up a small sack of gold, a magic wand, a lump of salt, and a flask of water. From the shelf she took down a golden ball and a gold cock and hen. Tying them all in a large kerchief, she set off with the prince as fast as they could go.

In a few hours the giant woke up hungry and went to the pot for his dinner. As soon as he tasted it, he spat it out. When he found nothing but rags and rubbish in the pot, he knew what had happened. He let out an angry bellow that shook the house, and rushed after them with long giant strides. It wasn't long before he saw them in the distance.

Maj threw down the lump of salt which immediately turned into a huge mountain. But that didn't stop the giant, who bored a tunnel right through the mountain.

Then Maj tossed out the water from the flask. The water became a broad sea, leaving the giant stranded on the other side.

Now they felt they were safe, so they set out at once for the prince's castle. But when they drew near, the prince insisted they must not walk up to the castle on foot like beggars. It was more seemly, he said, that Maj his betrothed should arrive in a coach. "Wait here but half an hour while I go home for the coach and horses in my father's stable. Then I can bring you properly to my father's castle."

Maj did not want him to do this. She had the power of foresight, and she knew further tests and danger lay ahead. The giant's revenge could follow them here. "Do not go back to the castle alone without me," she said. "Once you are there you will forget me and all that has happened between us."

"Don't worry, Maj," said the prince, "I could never forget you. I love you too dearly."

He was so eager to do her this honor that finally Maj assented. But she warned him, "You must go straight to the stables for the horses and return here. You must not speak to anyone. And above all, you must not eat anything. For if you do, we will suffer much grief and trouble."

The prince promised to do all this. He thought there was little chance he could forget his beloved Maj and their escape from the giant.

When the prince arrived at the king's castle, a great feast was being held, for his eldest brother had just been married. The castle was filled with a great crowd of people, and all were merrily rejoicing. The prince spoke to no one, nor would he eat anything. He went straight to the stables and harnessed the horses.

Now suddenly there appeared beside him a bewitching redhaired maiden who seemed to be one of the wedding guests, but she had, of course, been sent there by the giant.

"You must be hungry and thirsty after your journey," said she smiling. "If you won't eat any food, at least have a bite of my apple."

Hungry and thirsty he was—and bewitched as well—so he took a bite of the juicy apple. At once he forgot all about Maj. "I must be daft," he said. "Why am I harnessing a coach and horses?" He put them back in the stable and went along with the redhaired maiden to join the merrymaking.

The wedding celebration went on for weeks, as was the custom in those days. The prince was enchanted by the red-haired maiden, and at the end of this time he was easily persuaded to announce their betrothal.

In the meantime Maj had waited for the prince's return. When he did not come back, she feared he was under a spell and had indeed forgotten her. But she had not saved him from so many dangers only to abandon him now. She knew a few spells herself!

So she walked on until she came to a deserted, broken-down hut. Here she decided to stay, and at once set to work to clean it up. Then, remembering the giant's magic wand she had brought with her, she transformed the hut into a comfortable cottage with a garden of herbs and vegetables and a clutch of plump hens. Very quickly she became known around the countryside for her powers and skills.

The day for the wedding of the young prince to the red-haired maiden was set. But when the bride-to-be got into the coach, it broke down. The trace pin had broken; when it was repaired, it broke again. The wheel fell off; when it was replaced, it fell off again. No matter what was done, the coach could not be made to move. The bride sat inside raging with anger.

At the castle, the king was impatient at the delay. The guests, waiting for the coach to bring the bride, laughed at first to see it hopelessly stranded; then they grew uneasy. "The coach has a spell on it," they murmured.

The king's chamberlain, in charge of the procession, became more and more distraught. His wife, hearing the mur-

muring of the people, said to him, "Someone has cast a spell. There'll be no wedding unless you do something quickly. I've heard tell of a young woman at the edge of the forest who knows many charms. Send for her and she may be able to help you."

A messenger was dispatched at once. And thus it was that Maj was brought to the castle carrying a golden ball, a gold cock, and a gold hen. First she asked to see the prince who was to be married. Her request was granted.

Maj laid the gifts on the table before him. The gold hen pecked the golden ball over to the cock, and he with his beak returned it to her. Back and forth it rolled.

The prince was fascinated. "See how they share the ball, each with the other!"

"Yes," Maj replied, "just as you and I shared danger in escaping from the giant."

He looked at her in surprise for he did not recognize her. Then he picked up the golden ball. At once the giant's enchantment was broken. The prince exclaimed that he remembered everything, and they embraced each other happily.

The prince then told his father of his adventures, of his earlier betrothal to Maj, and how she had saved him. He said he loved her dearly and would marry no one but her, if she would still have him.

Maj said she would, for with her wisdom and his cheerful nature they were sure to live happily ever after. As for the red-haired maiden, she slid quickly out of the stranded coach and was never seen again in that country.

Variations of this Norse tale exist in Britain, Ireland, and Russia, places where the Norse settled over a thousand years ago, thus suggesting the antiquity of the story and theme. All the variations emphasize that the hero needs the heroine's wisdom in order to perform three very difficult tasks. G. W. Dasent's translation in *Norwegian Folk Tales* (1859) from the collection of Asbjornsen and Moe is the source for this retelling by the editor.

NOTES ON THE TALES

Folk tales are about human behavior in a world of magic and adventure. Underneath the surface story which entertains, there are usually one or more themes that illuminate the way the characters react, adding a deeper meaning to the tale. As noted in the *Introduction*, the tales teach moral and social values through the way people deal with one another and with the dilemma that confronts them.

The stories in this book have one thing in common: each has a heroine who demonstrates responsibility and resourcefulness in dealing with extraordinary events. Five of the tales are "romantic" in the most encompassing sense of the term. In these, the reader must suspend belief in the rational and the neatly logical, for the stories deal with the romantic concept of enchantments by other-world spirits. These stories also exalt the power of love between two people.

ROMANTIC TALES

In "Janet and Tamlin" and "The Laird's Lass," the heroines are not passive maidens awaiting the hero's choice. Both heroines actively make *their* choice of the loved one, and then overcome formidable obstacles and dangers to achieve their goals. Janet must wrest her lover from the Fairy Queen's power; the Laird's lass stands firm against an arranged marriage to win the husband of her choice.

The theme of the young man, maiden, or child captured by the fairy host is an old one in Celtic folklore, nor do all the tales end happily. A confrontation is usually required; and here Janet's courage is severely tested before she achieves her lover's freedom. The two tales also illustrate the differing attitudes of fairies and other-world creatures; some are selfish or malevolent, others are disposed to be friendly and to repay favors. That the Laird's lass entrusts her life and fate to the Wee Man is an act of unusual courage.

157

In both "The Enchanted Buck" and "The Black Bull of Norroway," the hero has been enchanted into an animal shape by supernatural forces of evil; he is doomed to exist in that shape until someone performs the specific rites which will break the enchantment and free him. The theme is of course familiar, but the heroines here do not sit in luxurious passivity until the spell is broken, as the heroine does in "Beauty and the Beast." Both girls look beyond the animal form to the spirit within and actively set about aiding the hero to break the enchantment. In "The Enchanted Buck," Lungile's specific ritual is relatively easy, although in terms of her culture it involves a great deal of courage and independence. Moving outside social and courtship customs, she accompanies a strange buck into alien territory, faces a monstrous ogre, and then is instrumental in freeing the young chief from enchantment.

The youngest sister in "The Black Bull" does not yearn for a conventional marriage of status as her elder sisters do. The strangeness of a black bull as suitor does not daunt her and, moved by love and affection, she is determined to help him break the enchantment. The tasks and obstacles are much more difficult than the ones Lungile faces, but perseverance and self-discipline enable her to succeed. In both stories the hero's fate can only be resolved by the heroine's active help.

"Kate Crackernuts" is another tale of spells and enchantment, and, like the story of the Black Bull, has Norse and Celtic elements. It is actually an integration of two stories—the spell put upon Anne, Kate's beloved foster sister, and the enchantment of the prince. The strong affection between the sisters is unusual for fairy tales. This affection, and the animal-head spell cast over one sister, parallel the Norse tale "Tatterhood." In both tales it is the active, resourceful sister who takes determined steps to seek out the supernatural forces needed to break the enchantment. Kate also succeeds in freeing the young prince from his deadly enchantment, but this is not a tale of young lovers. Whether Kate eventually marries the prince is immaterial to the story's basic theme; Kate defeats the malevolent forces and receives recognition and reward.

TALES OF RELATIONSHIPS

Six of the tales concern couples and the interaction of their behavior. The underlying themes emphasize the concept that mutual cooperation, as well as respect for each other's capabilities, are necessary to a couple's successful union.

The story of "Mastermaid" is in some respects "romantic," turning on the adventures of two young people in love—but on a deeper level, it comments on the positive way the two young people function as a couple. This is pointed out at the tale's end by the symbolic play of the golden hen and the cock with the ball, which signifies that only true partnership and cooperation can deal with the dangers of the world. Spells and enchantment are part of the plot, and it is the heroine, Maj, who enables the prince to escape the power of the giant. The young couple are more human and rounded in character than is usual in fairy tales—Maj, grave and serious; the prince, merry and impulsive. They are not a stereotyped fairy tale couple; and the cheerful message here is that heroines may indeed have more wisdom and knowledge than heroes, and a hero need not be traditionally heroic nor excel in all things to be loved.

"The Lute Player" makes use of neither magic nor enchantment. It is the tale of a queen's wisdom and achievement, as well as an approving comment on flexibility in the relationship of a couple. The queen is left to rule in the king's absence. She then has to make a wise decision concerning the best way to ransom and rescue her husband. Rather than impoverish the kingdom and its subjects in order to raise the ransom, the queen resorts to her skill as a musician to attain her purposes. Because minstrels were welcomed in both castles and monasteries, their musical talents providing passport and "safe conduct," the queen disguises herself as a minstrel and uses the customary reward given minstrels as the means of her husband's rescue. In both this story and "The Legend of Knockmany" there is an implied equality in the conduct of the couple's affairs, and the wife's skills are essential in solving the couple's dilemma.

"The Legend of Knockmany" is a parody of earlier heroic legends, with a lively humor that makes for a good tale. There is warm affection between Oonagh and Fin M'Coul. Fin, for all his superhuman strength, relies on Oonagh's imagination and practical wisdom to get him out of a tight corner. Her strategy succeeds brilliantly; the problem of Cucullin is disposed of permanently; and Oonagh ends up with her long-desired rearrangements in house and property.

In "The Prince and the Three Fates," a tale of the ancient Nile, the strength and determination of the princess enable her to save her husband's life. That she is instrumental in averting the doom predicted at his birth by fairies is unique—for most tales assume that the fate ordained by other-world spirits cannot be changed. "My wife," says the prince, gratefully, "has been stronger than my fate." This is, in its

159

way, a strongly positive theme, suggesting that the qualities and actions of human beings can alter and avert a fixed course of events. The princess is not a passive partner leaving the dilemma to her husband to solve; she takes decisive action to break the tragic prediction, and it is the prince's respect for his wife's capabilities that enables her to save him.

"Six Wives Who Ate Onions" is a folk tale built around a myth explaining the creation of star constellations. Anne Fisher, who adapted it for children, attributes the tale to the Western Mono Indians of California. Independent and strong-willed, the wives in this tale seek a new existence in the sky rather than submit to the husbands' ultimatum. A moral that may be inferred from this marital conflict is that flexibility and compromise are necessary for the successful sharing of lives.

"The Shepherd of Myddvai and the Lake Maiden" occurs in a number of variants in Wales; all of them attribute a family's medicinal lore to the wisdom of an earlier pagan deity, a local lake maiden or goddess. The mating of a local divinity with a mortal is an ancient theme. While in Greek myths such unions often had unfortunate results, in this tale of the Celtic lake maiden, the outcome is a blessing. The lake maiden settles quite easily into ordinary rural folk life and bestows the usual gifts of fertile crops and livestock. But she does state her own terms for the marriage, and the mortal husband keeps to their agreement. Their years together are contented ones. The brief glimpses we are given of the couple show the same mutual concern and respect found in the other tales of happy and successful unions.

TALES OF FAMILY AND COMMUNITY

Five of the tales deal with what could be called "family bonds" and, to some extent, a sense of community. All are from non-European areas. In the African tale "Unanana and the Elephant," a mother's courage and cleverness bring about the rescue of her children. Unanana's feat takes on the nature of a "tall tale," for she sets free not only her own children, but a vast number of other people and animals devoured by the elephant. The element of community is echoed in "The Giant Caterpillar," a tale from Uganda. When one woman's child is devoured, all the women of the village band together to kill the monster; they rescue the child and rid the village of the menace permanently.

"The Search for the Magic Lake" is a South American tale told by Inca Indians. Although the story is primarily about young Súmac's quest for magical water to cure an ailing prince, the warmth and strength of family bonds are clearly stressed. The success of the quest brings an offer of "adoption" by the royal family and the higher status that that implies. Súmac refuses the offer in order to return to her family; further, all that she asks is that her reward benefit her brothers and parents.

Although in this South American tale Súmac takes independent action to solve a problem, the part she plays in the quest is more passive than the one assigned to the heroines of similar European tales: she is given a fan which transports her at once to the magic lake; a forgotten flask is delivered to her; the feathered fan protects her from harm as she fills the flask, and it transports her back to the palace in a trice. Nevertheless, she is much more adventurous and brave than the majority of girls and women who appear in South American folk tale collections.

Heroines in the folk tales of pre-revolutionary China deferred to traditional family and social codes. In the tale "The Young Head of the Family," the heroine uses her wisdom and cleverness to achieve a position of power within that structure. Her abilities are recognized. Still, the rewards of her achievement are for the benefit of her family. In "Wild Goose Lake," we have a heroine, Sea Girl, who takes on the qualities valued in Communist China, while dealing with a dragon king of older mythology. The emphasis here is on the needs of the farm community, and Sea Girl's goal is to save the crops of the village.[1]

TALES OF WIT AND HUMOR

Cleverness is a valued quality in many folk tales; and it appears in varied forms. In "The Young Head of the Family," the cleverness or wit of the heroine is shown in both her quickness with riddles and her shrewdness with financial matters. "Clever Manka" also equates wisdom and intelligence with the solving of riddles. Manka's quick wits attract the earnest young burgomaster. However, he attempts to conduct their marriage on traditional patriarchal lines by ordering Manka not to help or cooperate in his duties but to remain in her own sphere as housewife. The lamentable result of this arrangement forces him to

[1]Wolfram Eberhard points out that this tale, collected by the Communist Chinese, stresses values they regarded as extremely important, and which "run counter to traditional Chinese values." See Notes (p. 222) and Introduction to *Folktales of China* by Wolfram Eberhard (University of Chicago Press, 1965). The Foreword by editor Richard Dorson gives detailed historical background.

value Manka's wisdom, and the ending points the way to a more equitable and successful marriage.

Norse tales often display an earthy humor and the peasant's irreverence for authority. The Norwegian farm lass in "The Squire's Bride" is both independent and clever. She refuses to be coerced into marriage and easily eludes the clumsy trap set for her. With a broad sense of humor, she repays the pompous Squire in his own coin, as he finds himself before the minister with a bay mare arrayed in bridal clothes.

In "Kamala and the Seven Thieves," the hardworking, resourceful Kamala not only makes the wasteland thrive, but cleverly preserves her earnings from the plotting of a band of thieves. There is sharp humor in Kamala's strategy. It differs from the verbal cleverness of Manka, and is more akin to the imaginative cleverness of Irish Oonagh and of the Norwegian farm lass.

TALES OF OLD WOMEN

Three of the tales in the collection portray cheerful, capable women. Endowed with practical wisdom and a sense of humor, they are remarkably unperturbed by the night demons they encounter. In "The Hedley Kow," the old woman is greatly entertained by the fearsome creature who has terrified the rest of the village folk. She accepts his changes of shape with good humor and acquires a companionable friend. The old farm woman of "The Hunted Hare" also lives alone, supporting herself with her livestock and crops. She meets the terrors of the monstrous hounds and headless horse with firmness, even defiance. The white hare, who is actually the enchanted White Lady, rewards her with abundance and prosperity.[2] The women in both tales are attractive and spirited, a fine counterbalance to the negative images of hags and crones found in many other folk and fairy tales.

The merry old woman in "Bucca Dhu and Bucca Gwidden" is also staunchly unafraid of supernatural creatures. The theme here is her right to live her own life in her own way. She refuses to conform to her son's staid, conventional ideas of what an old woman should be. Her individuality not only makes for an engaging tale, but also suggests to children that old people have the right to be themselves and enjoy life on their own terms.

[2]The White Lady in folklore is thought to date back to early local goddesses of fertility.

TALES OF INDEPENDENT WOMEN

Three generations of capable women turn up in the Japanese folk tale "Three Strong Women." This nonsexist tale makes its point in a gay, light-hearted manner. Tales of fantastic feats of strength are common in folklore, though few involve women. Although the story ends with the traditional rewards of gold and a desirable marriage partner, the elements that dominate the story are less familiar. Equality, mutual respect, and affection are evident in the relationship between the wrestler and the three women, as among the three women themselves. All four have expertise which they share with one another. The details of the ending take the theme of equality to its ultimate point, with delightful solemnity: the bride and groom take turns carrying each other up the hill. The strength of this tale lies in its clear affirmation of equality in relationships between people of different ages and sexes.

The remaining two tales present a pair of unusually self-reliant young heroines. In the tale from the Punjab, "Kupti and Imani," the two sisters are opposites. Kupti is passive and submissive—but later displays malicious jealousy. Imani is active, demanding of life the freedom to make her own choices. Poverty does not daunt her; she uses her skills and imagination, plus hard work, to build a serene and contented life, and eventually makes her own choice in marriage. The moral appears to be that submissiveness can lead to frustration and malice, while independence and rewarding work bring satisfaction and contentment.

The Norse tale "Tatterhood" also deals with the themes of individuality and nonconformity. On the surface, it is a rollicking tale of twin sisters, opposite in nature, but very fond of one another. The calf's-head bewitchment of the gentle, docile sister is similar to the enchantment described in "Kate Crackernuts." In both cases, the aggressive sister effects the cure. But "Tatterhood" is primarily the story of an unconventional young personage, disdainful of approval, of expected behavior, of pretty clothes. Her conception and birth are strange; from the beginning, there is a wild, elfin quality about her. She is endowed with unusual powers—but powers that are recognizably "good." Her mother, the queen, is pleased with the conventional twin, but throws up her hands in despair at Tatterhood. The king, however, seems to accept his daughter's strength and independence; he recognizes, when Tatterhood sets off with her sister for the outside world, that she is quite capable of sailing a ship unaided. Triumphing

163

over wicked trolls, Tatterhood saves her sister and, in a distant land, meets the prince who appreciates her individuality.

The dialogue between the prince and Tatterhood that occurs at the end of the tale is a form of testing. Tatterhood, who, if she chooses, can transform her goat into a fine steed and her own appearance into a socially acceptable one, makes the point that she is also free to live her life as she chooses. When the prince recognizes and accepts Tatterhood's sovereignty over herself, she knows that she has found a possible partner in marriage.

"Tatterhood" is one of the most interesting folk tales to come down to us. In the nineteenth century, Tatterhood was regarded as a social rebel, her behavior frowned upon. Her meek and mild, pretty twin sister was considered the ideal. In fact, the nineteenth century folklorist who retold the tale called Tatterhood a "hussy." But it is clear that Tatterhood is the primary character and the true heroine of her adventures.

All the tales in this collection were chosen for their positive themes, as well as for their resourceful heroines. Bringing these broad underlying themes into sharper focus can give the adult reader a clearer insight into "messages" in the tales that are sometimes overlooked; the attitudes and values implicit in these themes from centuries past have a special pertinence for our times.

SUGGESTED READING

Bauman, Hans. *Stolen Fire.* New York: Pantheon, 1974. Three of the tales in this collection are recommended: "Staver and Vasillissa," "Nana Miriam," and "Kara Khan's Daughter."

de Paola, Tomie. *Helga's Dowry.* New York: Harcourt Brace, 1977.

Gauch, Patricia. *Once Upon a Dinkelsbuhl.* New York: G.P. Putnam's Sons, 1977. Based on a German legend.

Harris, Christie. *Mouse Woman and the Mischief Makers.* New York: Atheneum, 1977. Based on Northwest Indian legends.

————. *The Mouse Woman and the Vanished Princesses.* New York: Atheneum, 1976. Based on Northwest Indian legends.

Herman, Harriet. *The Forest Princess.* Berkeley: Over the Rainbow Press, 1974.

————. *The Return of the Forest Princess.* Berkeley: Over the Rainbow Press, 1975.

Leodhas, Sorche Nic. "Lass Who Went Out at the Cry of Dawn." *Thistle and Thyme.* New York: Holt Rinehart and Winston, 1962. Based on Celtic folklore.

————. "The Woman Who Flummoxed the Fairies." *Heather and Broom.* New York: Holt Rinehart and Winston, 1960. Based on Celtic folklore.

Minard, Rosemary, ed. *Womenfolk and Fairy Tales.* Boston: Houghton Mifflin, 1975. A collection of traditional tales.

McGovern, Ann. *Half a Kingdom.* New York: Frederick Warne, 1977. Based on an Icelandic tale.

The Princess Book. Chicago: Rand McNally & Company, 1974. Five of the tales in this book are recommended: "The Princess Pella" by Ida Chittum, "Rosinda of the Red Ruby Ring" by Daphne Doward Hogstrom, "The Princess, the Prime Minister, and the Giant" by Helen Kronberg Olson, "The Patchwork Princess" by Betty Lacey, and "The Return of the Dragon" by Ester Hauser Laurence.

Williams, Jay. *The Practical Princess.* New York: Parents Magazine Press, 1969.

————. *Petronella.* New York: Parents Magazine Press, 1973.

Ethel Johnston Phelps
holds a master's degree in
Medieval Literature; she is co-editor
of a Ricardian journal and has published articles
on fifteenth-century subjects.
A native Long Islander, her activities
have included acting, writing, and directing in
radio drama and community theater.
Three of her one-act plays have been produced.

Pamela Baldwin Ford
is a noted children's book illustrator whose
work has been exhibited by the
New York Society of Illustrators. She graduated
from Paier School of Art in New Haven,
Connecticut, where she was the
winner of the National Women's Painting
Competition. She has taught drawing courses at
Paier for ten years and is currently the
vice-president of Fordesign, Inc.

The typefaces
used for the text of this book are
computer adaptations of Hermann Zapf's
Optima and H. Berthold AG's Korinna, while the
ornamental display face is Ringlet.
The text was typeset by Myrna Zimmerman, and it
was printed by R.R. Donnelley on Warren's
55# cream white Sebago paper.
The book was designed by Susan Trowbridge.

The Feminist Press offers alternatives in education and in literature. Founded in 1970, this nonprofit, tax-exempt, educational and publishing organization works to eliminate sexual stereotypes in books and schools, providing instead a new (or neglected) literature with a broader vision of human potential. Our books include reprints of important works by women, feminist biographies of women, and nonsexist children's books. Curricular materials, bibliographies, directories, and a newsletter provide information and support for women's studies at every educational level. Our inservice projects help teachers develop new methods to encourage students to become their best and freest selves. Through our publications and projects, we can begin to recreate the forgotten history of women and begin to create a more humane and equitable society for the future. For a catalogue of our publications, please write to The Feminist Press, Box 334, Old Westbury, New York 11568.

This book was made possible by the work of many people, including The Feminist Press Staff and Board. The Board, the decision-making body of the Press, includes all staff members and other individuals who have an ongoing relationship to The Feminist Press: Phyllis Arlow, Jeanne Bracken, Brenda Carter, Toni Cerutti, Ranice Crosby, Sue Davidson, Michelina Fitzmaurice, Shirley Frank, Merle Froschl, Barbara Gore, Brett Harvey, Ilene Hertz, Florence Howe, Paul Lauter, Carol Levin, Corrine Lucido, Mary Mulrooney, Dora Janeway Odarenko, Ethel J. Phelps, Elizabeth Phillips, Helen Schrader, Susan Trowbridge, Sandy Weinbaum, Sharon Wigutoff, Jane Williamson, and Sophie Zimmerman.

Many of the stories in *Tatterhood and Other Tales* have been recorded on cassette tape. The following three series are available from The Feminist Press. Please write to us for further information.

Series 1: Four Humorous Tales. Including "The Hedley Kow," "The Squire's Bride," "Kamala and the Seven Thieves," and "The Legend of Knockmany."

Series 2: Four Tales of Magic and Enchantment. Including "Janet and Tamlin," "The Black Bull of Norroway," "Tatterhood," and "Kate Crackernuts."

Series 3: Three Tales of Courage. Including "Kupti and Imani," "The Prince and the Three Fates," and "The Hunted Hare."